How to coach
TENNIS

How to coach
TENNIS

Bill Moss

WILLOW BOOKS
Collins
8 Grafton Street, London W1
1990

Willow Books
William Collins Sons & Co Ltd
London • Glasgow • Sydney • Auckland
Toronto • Johannesburg

First published 1990

Copyright © William Collins Sons & Co Ltd 1990

A CIP catalogue record for this book is available from the British Library.
ISBN 0 00 218322 6
paperback
ISBN 0 00 218372 2
hardback

Commissioning Editor: Michael Doggart
Senior Editor: Lynne Gregory
Designer: Peter Laws
Illustration: Susan Neale

This book was designed and produced by
Amanuensis Books Ltd
12 Station Road
Didcot
Oxfordshire
OX11 7LL

Originated, printed and bound in Hong Kong by Wing King Tong Co. Ltd

The pronoun 'he' has been used throughout and should be
interpreted as applying equally to men and women as appropriate.
It is important in sport, as elsewhere, that women and men should
have equal status and opportunities.

CONTENTS

INTRODUCTION

Tennis is an exciting game to play. It has no age limits. Men, women, boys and girls can enjoy its many features of play purely for exercise or for the fun of vying with one set of skills against another. The better one becomes, the more fun and enjoyment one gets from playing. If a player begins with the basic fundamentals then the rate of improvement can be much quicker.

This is where the coach enters the tennis arena, armed with the knowledge of the game, and with the understanding of how to use that knowledge; breaking the game down into easy learning parts, then putting it all back together again for the enjoyment of improved performance. He can help all players of any age to achieve their own specific goals and aspirations. Above all, he will strive to make them enthusiastic tennis players.

There is no greater pleasure for a coach than watching the players he has been coaching enjoying playing the game with new-found understanding and skills and being aware of what is required to improve their game. Very young children in particular become more confident and adventuresome, attempting shots they have seen the world's top players playing; a little success will have them ready and willing for the coach's next lesson.

The coach who remembers that young players want to play and understand the game, and not just learn the pure techniques of hitting tennis balls, will more than likely help them achieve this goal - and a successful coach he will be.

Bill Moss

Please note: Certain articles within this book are reproduced from copyright material from the L.T.A. *Training of Coaches Scheme* manual.

THE AUTHOR

Bill Moss has a distinguished record in competitive tennis; he was European Doubles Champion with Fred Perry in 1953 and three times British Professional Champion. From 1962 to 1982 he was National Coach for Scotland and is now consultant to the Scottish Lawn Tennis Association. Together with Charles Applewhaite and Kevin Livesey he has worked on the re-structuring of the .L.T.A. Training of Coaches Scheme, from elementary to professional coaching standards. Bill Moss is a long-standing member of the Professional Coaches Association and is now their President. For the last six years he has worked to develop a coaches training scheme in Hong Kong and, in particular, the training needed to coach juniors successfully.

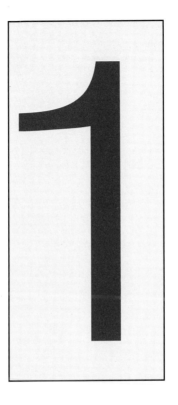

A COACH NEEDS TO BE...

A Coach Needs to be ...

Knowledgeable

You need to be knowledgeable about your sport, its structure, and the way the game is played. You must understand all the techniques and the skills needed to play well and know how to integrate the tactics and the strategies that the game dictates.

A high playing standard is not a prerequisite of being a sound teacher or coach, but you will need to demonstrate the basic strokes of the game, both statically (going through the motions of a shot without the ball) and in a rally, as well as be able to show what can be achieved with the stroke.

The Lawn Tennis Association runs a coaching award scheme and courses take place throughout the year. These courses contain all the relevant technical information.

> **Remember the KIS rule:**
> K - Keep
> I - It
> S - Simple

Sensitive

You should be understanding in your approach to beginners at the game, especially very young children. The tennis court is an enclosed arena and the gate is closed behind them. You want them to stay and feel relaxed, so create a happy atmosphere and make the lessons really enjoyable. Tennis in these early stages should be fun, and should continue to be so in a well-controlled learning situation.

Make every effort to understand your pupils' needs and what it is they wish to achieve during the lessons, and do everything possible to help them. Every little bit of success they have will motivate them further.

Inspiring

A good motivator makes all players believe they can achieve the goals they have set for themselves. You must have the ability to motivate yourself and achieve your own goals with the players. This is often very demanding. All players are different and while some have a genuine desire to learn, practice and achieve recognition, others may just want to be amused. Expect different attitudes to your lessons. Your success as a coach may well depend on your ability to satisfy all the players in the group, their goals and aspirations. Enthusiasm is an essential ingredient for success.

A good communicator

You have to sell your ideas and continually stimulate the players' interest in the game. Discuss with them the latest happenings in the tennis world.

A disciplinarian

Setting the ground rules of behaviour is important at the start. Players must know what is expected of them during the lesson. This discipline is especially important when working with children, for the safety of everyone.

You also need to encourage self-discipline in players within the group. You cannot keep an eye on everyone. Each player must practise between lessons to enhance their levels of performance.

Summary

The thoughtful coach will take the tools of his trade - his understanding of the game and of coaching - on court with him every session. They are as important as his tennis racket.

Beginners to tennis have come to learn about the game so these tools must be used intelligently. They will respond to the coach and give you the respect you deserve. Remember everything a coach does should be seen as an expression of his personality.

INTRODUCING THE GAME

Introducing the Game

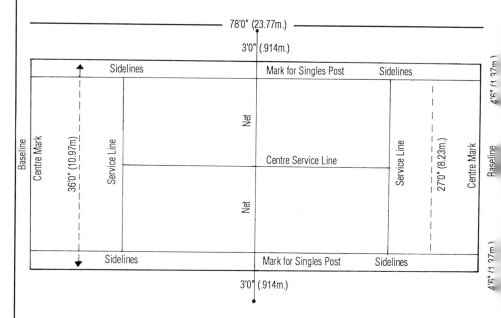

78'0" (23.77m.)

3'0" (.914m.)

Sidelines — Mark for Singles Post — Sidelines

Net

Centre Service Line

Net

Sidelines — Mark for Singles Post — Sidelines

3'0" (.914m.)

Baseline · Centre Mark · 360" (10.97m.) · Service Line

Service Line · 27'0" (8.23m.) · Centre Mark · Baseline

4'6" (1.37m.)

4'6" (1.37m.)

Dimensions of a tennis court

There is no better way to introduce the game of tennis to a group of novice players than to have two very good players come along to the session and play a tennis match for them. Close to the action, the spectators can appreciate more the speed of the ball travelling between the players and the speed and athletic movements needed to reach the ball and return it back into the court. They will see the different movements the racket makes during service, forehands and backhands, volleys and smashes, and the sheer excitement good rallies generate. With some guidance the children will be able to follow the tactics being used to win points, games and the match.

You will spot a number of things from watching the good players in action - not only their approach to hitting the ball, but their feeling for the game, their different personalities and approach to the game and, above all, their enjoyment of the experience.

You can then use your knowledge of the game to make a simple analysis of what was being demonstrated to talk your pupils through the game you have watched together.

Simple analysis

Movements

Analyze the way that both players move around their open half of the court retrieving their opponent's shots. Note the alert readiness of both players who can, from a good position on the court, move quickly to the right place at the right time maintaining their balance to deal with a difficult return of shot.

Racket work

Watch the way that both players use the racket, and the rhythmic nature of the movements they make when playing forehands and backhands (groundstrokes) with a sawing action. Compare these with the throwing action of the service and smash, and the punching action of the volley.

Consistent returns

This comes from a combination of good anticipation of returned ball position with the way a player relates to the ball before the strike. Comment on the players' ability to consistently control the racket when playing groundstrokes, serving, smashing and volleying, thus controlling the speed, flight and direction of the ball.

Tactics

With their mastery of the three previous points, the two good players reveal their tactical approach. Errors occur in general when players are under pressure. With this in mind, both players aim to keep the ball in play consistently returning into empty spaces of the court and making their opponent run around. Each player strives to maintain control from the back of the court as well as opening up attacking possibilities with net play.

This analysis should then prompt a discussion between the group and the pupils which should further stimulate their interest in the game, and will hopefully make them determined to learn to play as well.

That is exactly what you are going to let them try to do. Arrange games. You have no standards to go by yet, so pair them off by age and size and let them play. Encourage them and use the two good players to help. Don't expect miracles, but if they manage to copy anything at all from the demonstration then they are already better players. From now on it is all up to the coach.

Summary

Watching good players in action is stimulating. It must be remembered that many players, particularly young children, may never have seen good players in action in the flesh or even understand how a match is played. Without this basic knowledge coaching is meaningless. Players must know what they are striving to achieve.

Through simple analysis of the playing standards of the group in the games that follow the demonstration, the coach can discover what his group needs to work on in the lessons ahead.

BASIC SKILLS

Basic Skills

Basic skills include the fundamentals of tennis strokes and give a sound foundation for the development of the more sophisticated skills necessary to raise the standard of play. These fundamentals are deep-rooted in the games of the world's best players.

If nothing more than the basic skills were efficiently executed, new players would be able to play the game of tennis to a very respectable level. As a coach you should never under estimate the importance of the following basic skills:

• Ball sense and movement
• Consistently finding the hitting area and
  contact point
• Competent use of the racket head
• Linked fundamentals
• Striking the ready position.

Ball Sense and Movement

A highly-developed ball sense is essential in order to play well. It is the ability to coordinate what you see with what you do: that is, to coordinate your reaction to the moving ball with what you see. Every improving step a player makes puts his ball sense under more pressure, increasing the demands for quicker and better movements around the court.

The first thing beginners have to cope with is the speed of the ball and the way it bounces. Concentration and alertness will help them anticipate an opponent's play. Experience will teach them that a good position on the court also helps them reach the ball with ease and put it back into play.

In the early stages of learning the game, young players may experience difficulties which actually stem from an under-developed ball sense. The ball may seem too lively, the court too big an area to cover, the net too high and the racket too big and heavy. Young players particularly may feel frustrated and their spirits may be dampened.

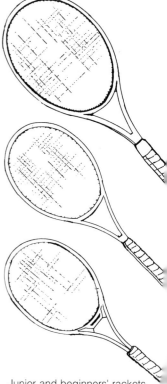

Junior and beginners' rackets (above), in comparison with the standard adult racket (top) have enlarged heads to produce a greater hitting area and shorter handles for added manoeuverability.

Short tennis is a fairly recent innovation which can help to restore children's flagging enthusiasm. Details of short tennis will be given later in Chapter 4.

Ball-sense activities are a wonderful area for the coach to show his inventiveness. Here are a few sample exercises:

• Two players throw and catch the ball without a bounce. Begin with easy throws then increase movements forwards, backwards and sideways. Encourage jumping to catch high balls.

• Use two balls for the same exercise - even quicker responses are needed.

• Use the same exercises but catch after one bounce.

• Throw the ball over the net using the short tennis court. This helps in the understanding of the simple tactical ploys of winning points.

• Use the racket to continually bounce the ball on the court. Progress to bouncing the ball on the racket into the air and then bouncing using the edge of the racket.

• Toss the ball from racket to racket on the full court. Start close together then move further away in stages.

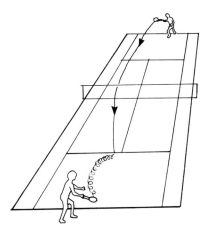

When a groundstroke is played, the ball has two flight paths.

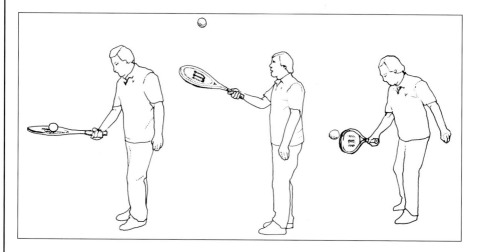

The bounce, toss and hit exercise is very effective in developing ball sense.

• Same exercise with one bounce.
• Play a game over the net, each player in turn collecting the ball on the strings, dropping it off the strings for one bounce, then hitting it over the net. Use a simple, scoring system.
Note: Use tennis balls or different rackets and sponge balls depending on ability.

The Hitting Area and Contact Point

The second of the basic skills is using ball sense to develop a sound hitting method through correct positioning.

To do this successfully, each type of stroke should be played using the same movement pattern. This ensures that the ball appears in the same place in relation to the body at impact each and every time.

By establishing and understanding this hitting area, beginners are able to develop a consistent hitting method which lends itself to better control of the ball and its direction.

Forehand: The hitting area/
contact point

The groundstrokes

In the groundstrokes, there is a demand for an understanding of
the hitting area and contact point throughout the playing of the
shots:

1. The ball should be struck at a height somewhere between the
knee and waist. This is physically the most natural level for
playing groundstrokes.

2. The ball should be struck at the side and slightly in front of the
body.

3. The ball should be struck at a comfortable distance from the
body.

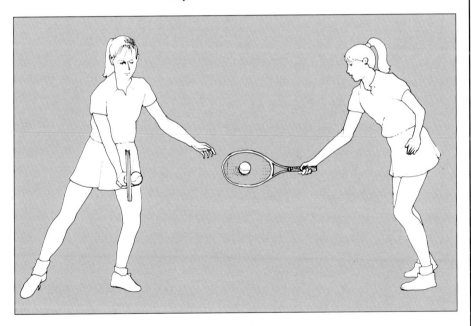

Backhand: The hitting area/ contact point

Younger children and older beginners will improve their chances of being able to rally with a partner if they hit the ball after the top of the bounce, but should not be discouraged from playing the ball before this point so long as they keep a comfortable distance away from the ball. The falling arc of the ball after the bounce makes for a better, more controlled forward swing.

Sound play is achieved if the above three points are observed so emphasis should be placed on:
• Watching the ball very carefully
• Creating the time to produce a shot by developing a more methodical positioning to the ball
• A more balanced position.

The following exercises are examples of progressive practices for developing an understanding of the hitting area and contact point:

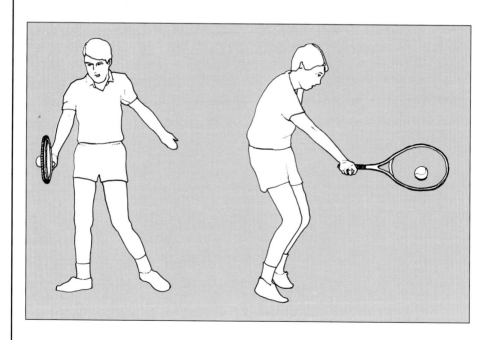

• Using the palm of the hand, swing the hand towards the ball and catch it at a comfortable distance from the body between waist and knee height.
• Using the sponge ball it is possible to hit it with the hand.
• Vary the height of the fed ball to encourage movement backwards and forwards for correct positioning.
• Simple rallying in pairs. Start with the sponge ball, progress towards the same exercise with 'soft' tennis balls; extend a rope across the court above net height (badminton stands can be used). Use hoops for additional enjoyment of this exercise.
• Make use of the tramlines to keep a comfortable distance away from the ball. Use hoops for the feeders to target the balls for the striker.
• Get young players to bounce the ball with the racket , one behind the other, along outside tramlines to centre of the baseline. Feet behind the baseline, ball ahead of the baseline a comfortable distance away from the body, hit the ball over the net. This encourages correct positioning with the ball in front and at the side.

Two-handed backhand:
The hitting area/contact point

Service

In a game, the service is the only time a player is stationary. It is also the only time a player is in control of all of the action. It is important that all the players appreciate how important this stroke opportunity is to their game, and that the placement of the ball is crucial.

The hitting area and contact point are again critical to the shot:

1. The ball should be struck at maximum hitting height.
2. The ball should be struck slightly forward of the body and towards the target.
3. The ball should be struck slightly to the right hand side of the body.

Service: The hitting area/ contact point

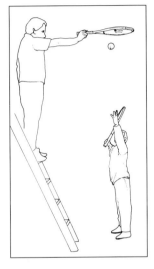

Placing the ball for the
beginner to play.

Players should work at all three points of ball placement. Only when all three work as one unit within the whole action will sound placement of the ball be achieved.

Planning a sound position for striking the ball around the three dimensions will help to develop:
1. A more methodical approach
2. A grooved stroke
3. A more natural throwing action
4. Better control and direction
5. Better balance
6. More power.

The following exercises are examples of possible practices to help in the placement of the ball:
1. The held target - partner stands on a bench holding out a hoop, or racket with no strings, as a target. Player practises hitting target with thrown ball.
2. Placing the ball - the player places the ball in the air with one hand and practises, minus racket, hitting or 'shadowing' it with the other.
3. Using the racket - player places ball in the air and makes correct racket movement without actually hitting the ball. If placed properly, the ball should fall back naturally into the player's throwing hand.

Volleys

In the volley situation the young players are nearer to the opponent who is hitting the ball. This will mean quicker responses to get into a sound position from which to volley. The hitting area and contact point now only cover two areas:
1. The ball should be struck in front of the body.
2. The ball should be struck slightly to the side of the body, but nearer to the body than for groundstrokes.

Planning a sound position for striking the ball around these two areas will help the players to develop:
1. A more methodical shot
2. A grooved shot
3. A firmer shot
4. Better balance
5. Better control and power.

The following are examples of exercises to help position the ball for volleying:
1. Catching the ball with the hitting hand, with the open palm simulating the racket head.
2. With a partner simulate a volley rally by tossing a ball to one another and catching with racket hand above net height (shoulder height).
3. Repeat the same two exercises with the racket. Use a sponge ball first; progress to soft tennis ball.

Summary

Making maximum use of ball sense is the only way to position the ball correctly for hitting. Quick responses and good movement will lead to sound, smooth and rhythmical action with the racket.

It is important that the coach studies his young players carefully to develop sound positions for groundstrokes, serves and volleys. Simple exercises establish the understanding they require to broaden their racket skills.

Volleys
Top right: Forehand volley The hitting area/ contact point
Bottom right: Backhand volley The hitting area/ contact point

Use of the Racket Head

Having got to grips with reaching the ball at the right time to perform a simple racket skill, the skill must be repeated often and grooved into the beginners.

The swing movement in the forehand drive.

The essential differences in the use of the racket head for the range of strokes are:
• Groundstrokes - The racket head should be swung
• Service - The racket head should be thrown
• Volley - The racket head should be punched or blocked.

Groundstrokes

1. Players must have the maximum time to hit the ball, and use a smooth take-back of the racket. Early preparation for the shot is vital.
2. The falling ball from the top of the bounce encourages the correct forward path of the racket head.
3. Developing an effective swing of the racket head is only achieved by having a good hitting area and contact point.
4. Use a swinging racket action.

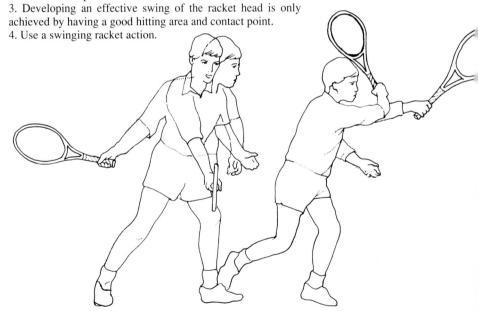

The throwing movement in the service.

All these points apply to beginners whether they use one hand or two for a particular shot.

Get the players to let their eyes follow the path of the racket head from backswing to follow-through a number of times. Slowly they will begin to feel the swinging action.

Service

1. Adopt a comfortable but strong throwing stance.
2. To achieve the correct racket head movement, the ball must be towards the target, in front and slightly to the racket side of the body, and at an effective hitting height.
3. Develop an explosive position of the racket behind the head.
4. Use a throwing action of the racket head at the ball.

Volleys

1. A player in a position to volley will be closer to the opponent and will therefore have less time to prepare than he would for groundstrokes.
2. Contact should be made with the ball only slightly to the side, but always in front of the body.
3. The player should keep firm control of the racket, little backswing is required, and use a short blocking or punching action.

The punch movement of the volley.

Summary

Having introduced the use of the racket head, the coach may find beginners hitting the ball too hard, particularly in groundstroke rallies. Encourage controlled use of the swing, but with a firm contact. It will need a lot of effort on the coach's part to combine the coaching of ball sense with an ability to adopt a sound position to use the racket smoothly. Enjoyable exercises in all these areas will help the beginner to master this.

Linked Fundamentals

Now that the coach has laid the foundation of becoming a more efficient player, he must now be thinking of quality of movement, positioning for hitting the ball, and the use of the racket head. He must also work at developing the linked fundamentals that are the basis of sound strokeplay.

The following fundamentals have an important role to play in improving strokeplay:
1. Watching the ball
2. Footwork
3. Balance
4. Control of the racket swing, throw and punch
5. Control of the racket face.

Watching the ball

Every player watches the ball when he plays tennis, but the very good player watches it more carefully and reacts more precisely than the average player. Young players should be encouraged to watch the ball with care, following:
• The trajectory of the shot
• The probable landing place of the ball
• The place they will need to move to in order to play a comfortable shot
• Any spin on the ball that might affect their previous observations.

The beginners have got to learn how to sift all this information to enable them to achieve their objective. It will require tremendous concentration and application to raise their technical skills.

The coach can emphasize these points by organizing an exercise in which the beginners study the flight of a series of balls he hits down the court. Ask them about the height of the ball over the net after every shot.

Follow this up by hitting a ball down the court with one of the players in a receiving position just behind the baseline. The player will allow the ball from the coach to bounce twice (there is no attempt to hit the ball) and then place a ball on the court where the shot first bounced and a second ball on the spot where the ball bounced a second time. The coach should talk about the distance between the two balls, then show them that the most comfortable hitting position is nearer the second ball. Many beginners rush towards the ball on its first bounce. Experimenting with spin in this same exercise will stimulate interest. An introduction to strokes with spin follows in Chapter. 8.

Footwork

Tennis is a game of explosive movement around a playing area (singles) of 39' x 27' (11.88 x 8.23 metres) which may not seem very large to cover. However, it generally takes only two or three seconds for a ball to travel from one baseline to the other, so there is very little time in which to prepare and play. Good, quick footwork is therefore essential. In tennis there are two major types of footwork:
1. The movement to the ball which must be fast and explosive, enabling the player to reach the ball in good time;
2. The small adjustment of footwork when the player has reached the ball. This enables the player to set his position to the ball correctly.

Coaches and players should study good players in action, focusing attention on the two types of footwork necessary for good positioning to the ball. Most of the good players' hard work goes unseen, especially their footwork.

Balance

In every ball game balance and poise are important factors. In tennis there are two areas of balance to consider:
1. The balancing position at the end of a movement prior to the hit;
2. The balance required during the hit.

When a player moves very quickly from one position to another and then slows down quickly, there is always the possibility of losing balance. A player must learn the art of moving quickly to the ball and retaining a balanced position prior to hitting the ball. However there is still fifty per cent of the work to be done, as it is fundamental to the success of the shot that as the player begins to swing the racket, balance must be retained to control the swing and direction of the shot. Loss of balance at this point will certainly mean an uncontrolled shot. Tennis is a game of controlled balance.

Control of the racket movement

The two previous fundamentals were specific to movement: that is, reaching the ball balanced for play. Now a player must move the racket in the most efficient way to hit the ball. A player must think in terms of the speed of the swing, angle of swing and the overall shape of the swing. It will help the player to visualize the racket as a natural extension of the arm.

In the swing there are two distinct phases of movement. The first is the controlled backswing, which should prepare the player well for the second and most important phase, the hitting or forward swing. These phases should be linked together in a rhythmical and efficient manner to achieve a successful shot. There are many different shots and therefore many different movements of the racket (swing, throw and punch), so it is important to give young players a clear mental picture of the shot being attempted. There are major differences, for example, between a forehand volley and a backhand lob. The first is a short, sharp, generally downward movement; the second is a slow, long, upward swing. To be successful the coach must be sure that his beginners understand these different racket-movement patterns.

Control of the racket face

All the fundamentals have been leading up to this, the most important time - contact with the ball. This moment will decide whether or not the ball is going to clear the net and remain in play. The ball is only in contact with the racket for three milliseconds, so the contact must be exactly right the first time. The moment the ball is struck, the angle created by the racket face at impact point will determine the ball's flight off the racket face. A particular method of holding the racket for each shot (the grip) should be selected early, and any grip change should be accomplished in the early part of the backswing.

Very young children should be advised to adopt simple basic grips in the early stages of development. An Eastern, shake-hands grip should be used for the forehand and will probably also be used in the service. For the backhand, there will be a slight movement of the hand to the left from the Eastern grip forehand. If beginners are keen to use the two hands on the backhand, the left hand will form an Eastern grip above the right hand.

Eastern grip

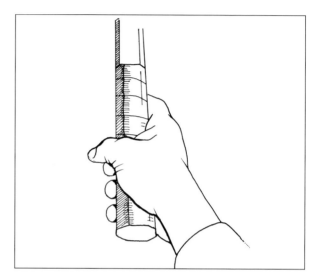

Western grip

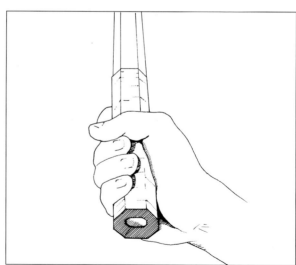

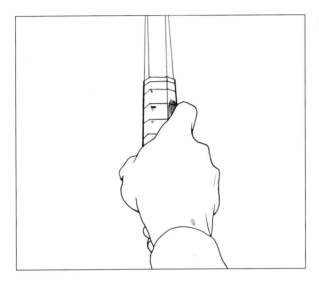

Grip for single-handed backhand

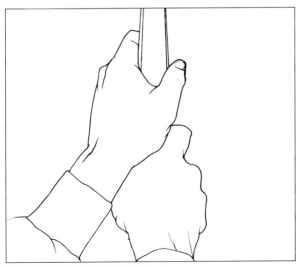

Grip for two-handed backhand

Two-fisted grip

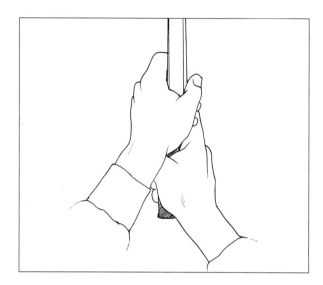

The Ready Position

Every activity should start from a position of readiness, and after each shot is played the player should return to a ready position to continue the rally.

Groundstrokes

Strike a relaxed position:
- Feet shoulder-width apart, the body bent over the racket head with the knees slightly bent;
- Eyes concentrated on the opponent;
- Standing three to four feet (a metre) behind the baseline when playing from the back of the court;
- The racket supported with the free hand.

Service

Stand in a comfortable sideways position:
- In a strong, throwing stance;

- With both feet behind the baseline;
- Feet about shoulder width apart;
- Hands pointing towards the target;
- Ball and racket together at the beginning of the movement.

Volley

Remember that this stroke is an action in which beginners are close to their opponents so encourage a starting position in which:
- The player looks alert and springy , and has the racket supported by the spare hand and held above the height of the net;
- The feet are shoulder-width apart, with the body bent over towards the target and the knees slightly bent;
- Eyes are focused on the opponent;
- The player is positioned roughly seven to eight feet (two metres) from the net, near the centre service line.

Volley : The ready position

Summary

The linked fundamentals should be seen as putting polish on the earlier basic skills, with the player's movement around the court becoming not only quicker but smoother and rhythmical. More consistent correct positioning to the ball will lead to better balance before and during the hit and, because of this, racket work will become repetitive and useful. Playing rallies should be the goal of every beginner.

Once this stage is reached, it could be a good time for the coach to have the two very good players back again to give another demonstration of play. The beginners' lessons to date will have given them more understanding of the basic skills, so they will view the playing of the game differently. The linked fundamentals can be studied in detail while the two good players continue to play.

Already there is a great deal to remember and very young children should only be given one or two items to practise at the most. It is very tempting for the coach to demand far too much from these younger players, so remember that it is wise to take one's time.

SHORT (MINI) TENNIS

Short (Mini) Tennis

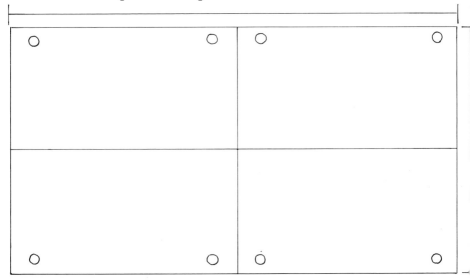

Short (mini) tennis
The use of a full court to accomodate eight players of the game.

As a coach you are probably aware of the difficulties that very young children encounter with the basic skills, and how they are not always of their own making. One of the biggest problems is that the tennis ball is very lively and smaller beginners find it difficult to cover the whole court in order to reach and return the ball. This may have the effect of dampening the players' initial enthusiasm.

In Sweden, extensive specialist research came up with the answer: short tennis, a proportionally-reduced version of the full scale game that is realistic and fun.

The main reason for its success is the ball which is made of sponge rubber, and slightly larger than a normal tennis ball. This ball travels more slowly through the air and the slower, lower bounce gives young beginners much more time to play their strokes. Short tennis bats made of plastic can be used although in many countries shorter, lightweight, strung rackets are favoured because they make it easier for the player to progress from the sponge ball to a slightly faster ball.

The court size is reduced to roughly badminton court size,

although when the game was introduced in Sweden, there were no strict rules about court size. The playing area has a lower net height of just 0.85 metres, and until specific nets were made for short tennis, benches, chairs, or a rope across the court were used. Almost any space that is flat can be used for short tennis.

The benefits of short tennis are great. Eight to sixteen players can actually play a game on one tennis court. This makes it possible for the coach to help young players in a smaller area and watch over their young players' development. For the players, it reduces the frustration of aimlessly chasing a lively ball on a big court and lets them develop the game where a point is won only when the ball can be kept going over the net many times. This leads to an awareness of the tactics and concentration that are required. Determination and the physical abilities of stamina and speed become important factors, as does the need for an improved quality of strokeplay. The basic skills previously described are also easier to implement because of the soft ball.

There is less of the tension and panic often seen with children playing the full-size game. When they are relaxed and enjoying rallies, children get a feel for movement around the court and the use of the racket much more quickly than in the standard game. Results are immediate, with the competitive spirit shining through as a chance of success becomes a reality. Short tennis is fun, and fun is exactly why children new to the game want to play it.

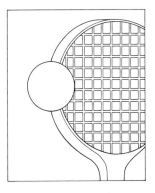

Short (mini) tennis equipment
Tennis bats are plastic and just over half the size of a normal tennis racket. The ball is made of soft, absorbent foam.

Basic Rules

1. The best of three games constitutes a match.
2. The game is played up to eleven points. If the score reaches ten-all, two clear points are then needed to win.
3. The service changes hands every two points, the server having two attempts to place the ball in court.
4. The service from the right-hand court should be placed over the net in the opponent's left-hand court.
5. The normal rules of tennis are enforced.

SHORT (MINI) TENNIS

The game was introduced on a small scale to Great Britain in 1980 but its value was such that it was encouraged nationally by the Lawn Tennis Association. It also received an enthusiastic reception from educationalists. Primary and middle school teachers in particular, quickly recognized that short tennis is an excellent means of introducing a pupil to a simple bat-and-ball activity, and as such, enables them at a very early age to learn a skill which can form the basis of further ball-sport games including tennis.

Remember that it is a lead to tennis and as such should be used intelligently. Interchange the sponge ball for a soft tennis ball for controlled specific practices of the basic skills, then back to the sponge ball for game play. In this way each will complement the other.

There is another development from short tennis. Sweden has introduced a 'middle' game, this time using a ball similar to a tennis ball, but very soft; you can squeeze the sides of the ball together. It is quicker through the air, but because of its softness, the ball bounces at a 'kind' height with a slow bounce.

The ball is used a great deal in Hong Kong. Their coaches work with young players who have mastered the basic skills, but still find the tennis court and lively ball too difficult to maintain these skills. This ball does give the coach more scope in progressing the young players in the basic strokes.

With the aid of sponge balls, intermediate and soft tennis balls, the coach can bring his young players to the real game in a controlled way, maintaining great enthusiasm, fun and enjoyment.

Stages of progression

Listed below is a possible sequence of progression for taking
children from short (mini) tennis towards the full-sized game.
These ideas are suitable for:
• Teaching the individual
• Teaching groups
• Games and exercises
• Competitions
• The game itself.

Court size	Equipment	Notes
Short tennis	• Short tennis/plastic bats. • Indoor foam ball.	• Ideal game for playing indoors.
Short tennis	• Short tennis/plastic racket. • Outdoor short tennis ball. • Foam ball if not too windy.	• Play can be indoors or outdoors.
Short tennis	• Junior tennis racket . • Outdoor short tennis ball.	• Play can be indoors or outdoors. Make sure tennis racket is of suitable size.
Modified tennis court - lower net; possibly service area only.	• Junior tennis racket. • Outdoor short tennis ball.	• The modifications to the court etc should be related to age and degree of success being achieved.
Full-size tennis court.	• Tennis racket of appropriate size for pupil. • Outdoor short tennis ball.	• Make sure pupils are familiar with tennis court • Use tennis scorings.
Full size	• Tennis racket of appropriate size for pupil. • Tennis ball (very soft).	• Stress importance of good feeding. Use tennis scoring.

Summary

The coaching of ball games has come a long way in recent years with a better understanding of the problems beginners have - especially children - with mastering the basic skills.

Short tennis without doubt has changed the learning process of tennis drastically. The speed and bounce of the ball, almost impossible to control unless fed by an understanding senior for a young child to hit, is now a thing of the past. By cutting down the size of the playing area and making equipment easy to handle at an early age there is no need to wait to grow up before you can play. The sponge ball, the airless tennis ball and very soft tennis ball leave frustration behind. Rallies that were once unthinkable between two young players, are now a regular occurrence with a soft ball. Equally, the racket is now made shorter and lighter to suit the young beginner. Children can now control the racket movements which, in turn, means they can begin to learn all the techniques that tennis involves.

Groups of children working together are also safe from the danger of uncontrolled tennis balls, always a worrying factor for coaches and teachers, and there is now more room for freedom of individual expression.

DEMONSTRATIONS AND FEEDING

Demonstrations and Feeding

Demonstrations

Much of the success of very young children stems from a coach's ability to demonstrate clearly all the basic skills that are tutored in the lesson. Movement, positioning and hitting are the obvious skills, but when working with children in a class, cooperation is also a vital ingredient. For this reason, demonstration of feeding requirements is necessary so that one player can cooperate with another to fulfil a task set by the coach.

Any demonstration should speak for itself. The whole of the activity should take place before any detailed explanations are given. Finish with a full demonstration. Only the briefest explanations should be used, and the demonstration should be repeated several times.

Within the practices that follow all demonstrations, the coach should play an active role, taking over from each feeding player in the class, and the place of the striking players. Be one of the class. In this way the coach not only helps each individual but keeps the original picture of his demonstration alive.

The following points are important to remember when demonstrating:

1. Show the whole, the detail and the whole again.
2. Make your demonstrations good, no matter how simple the skill.
3. One demonstration is never enough.
4. Use brief verbal explanation with key words and phrases.
5. Place your class in the best possible position to see the demonstration.
6. Be prepared to move your class to see the demonstration from a different viewpoint.
7. Identify and demonstrate the relationship of the ball, the racket and the body to perform the required stroke.
8. Remember, movement is a requirement of tennis. Demonstrate with movement, even if it is only a few steps.
9. Remember, as coach the class looks up to you so don't disappoint them. Give them the best possible picture you can.

Feeding for Success

Once a coach's demonstration has taken place and the class is practising the skill, it will be the feeding skills of the coach that will bring about early success.

These young players working to improve their tennis skills need time: time to think about the points that have been presented to them and time to put their thoughts into action. Young players cannot succeed if the ball is not fed to them correctly. Feeding balls at a pace well within the capacity of each young player will allow them to achieve the task set by the coach. Hitting balls consistently over the net boosts confidence and arouses a greater interest in learning to play well - success is motivating.

The coach's feeding skills will need to be practised, by hand and with the racket. A coach will use a wide range of feeding methods, from the most simple one of dropping balls to be hit, to the rallying of a ball with an individual. It is the playing standard of the player that dictates the feeding methods to be used. In working with a group of young players, the coach may wish to control all the feeding, but that means young players waiting in line to hit the ball - this could lead to loss of interest of the very young player. The coach must therefore encourage young players within the group to work with one another, and learn to cooperate with one another to achieve success. They will use the simple hand feeding method initially, but should develop to the dropped ball and hitting method of feeding. The use of hoops on the court can help the feeder to 'target' the ball accurately for their partner to practise the techniques of groundstroke play.

It must be remembered that young children prefer to be in the position of hitting, so making them enjoy the role of feeder is quite a task. Sometimes a competitive situation between pairs, where their hitting successes are added together, encourages more control when feeding but, in general, short hitting periods, governed by a certain number of balls to be played, works equally well.

Groundstrokes

Feeding by hand

1. Standing at the side of the player, who is positioned ready to hit the ball, drop the ball vertically for the player to hit. This is a good method for grooving the correct hitting position and the height of the ball. It also encourages the correct swing and control of the racket face, and allows easy communication with the player.

2. Standing at the side of the player, who will be in ready position, toss the ball in the air vertically. This will give the player time to prepare the backswing and play either a forehand or backhand. Allows easy communication with the player.

3. Feeding the ball underarm from the net gives the ball the same trajectory as if it were being played with the racket. Using progressive feeding, movement forwards, backwards and sideway, can be encouraged while maintaining the technical skills of the practice. Linking forehand play with recovery to a ready position and then playing backhand, leads to a rally situation.

4. Feeding a series of balls from the net to produce a rally of forehands and backhands with recovery to a ready position after each hit of the ball.

Feeding with the racket

1. Feeding with the racket after the ball has bounced from the mid-court, and back from the back of the court. The bounce of the ball alerts the player that the ball is about to be fed. This method of feeding needs good control of the ball to place it accurately time and time again for repetitive practice. Always try to feed each ball with sound technical form. This keeps the demonstration picture on view for players to see.

2. With the racket, produce a rally. The ability to take the speed off a young player's shots is very important. Rallying and even playing a game with a young player, requires a higher standard of ability in the player and should introduce him to a tactical appreciation of strokeplay.

Volleys

Feeding by hand and racket

All the suggested methods of feeding for groundstrokes will be used when practising volleys. Feeding must be accurate and in the early stages it is important to feed the ball so that young children can hit the ball at shoulder height. They achieve much greater success at this shoulder-high position. Feeding with the racket to a volleyer is quite difficult, so it would be better to use the soft pressureless ball and this should certainly be used when young players are feeding one another within a class session.

Young children are a little unsure and nervous at the net, and making them confident is essential - keep the ball well to the side of them, and keep the ball as near to shoulder height as possible.

A feeding method for the service

The placement of the ball in the air when serving is an important part of serving successfully, and young children in particular have great difficulty working both hands together. The coach can feed the placement of the ball for them.

Stand at the side of the player, and synchronize the player's backswing with the placement of the ball. It takes a little time and practise to get the timing right between the coach and the player - but it does work and the success of hitting the serve gives a lot of satisfaction. The realization that placing the ball correctly gives a better chance of success makes them practise the important part of serving more readily.

Problems of feeding

1. The ball travelling too fast for the ability of the young player.
2. The ball being fed too close to the young player.
3. The ball bouncing too high or too low for the young player.
4. Putting too much spin on a racket-hit ball can be confusing for a young player.
5. Placing feeder and striker either too close or too far away from one another - a comfortable distance for both is important.

Summary

There is absolutely no doubt at all that the two most valuable assets a coach has are his demonstration skills and the quality of his feeding.

The ability to give a clear visual picture of any task, which should be repeated at intervals during a coaching session, is important. It is useful for beginners to see clearly how the task is executed and how effective the result of the execution can be.

The success the young beginners achieve will now come from very good feeding related to ability and, once success is achieved, sound feeding almost on its own encourages a higher standard of performance. It very definitely breeds confidence and understanding.

Although one expects a coach to feed a ball by any method, his greatest task will be to get his young players to feed well to one another. A coach in schools usually spends more time working with groups on court, and successful group coaching is dependent on cooperation.

Make the most of equipment, to breed success in demonstrations and feeding. Use soft balls that make the bounce easy to cope with and reach a height that is comfortable to hit. Use hoops to target and encourage good feeding.

BASIC STROKE TECHNIQUES

Basic Stroke Techniques

The phrase 'basic strokes' may give the impression that there is a rigid formula for strokeplay, but this is not strictly true. Players reflect their own personality through their interpretation of these techniques, and although the coach should appreciate this, he should ensure that players understand the importance of sound basic techniques as a foundation upon which successful play is built.

A player needs sound technique supported by advanced racket skills to cover the three important phases of the game:
1. Defence
2. Attack
3. Counter-attack.

He must know the important role played by spin in each of these phases. He must not only practise these skills but also understand their purpose.

Coaches understand these factors because they study class players who generally stay well in control of any situation and demonstrate the principles of sound stroke production. Their strokeplay remains secure even in the most difficult of pressure situations.

Young beginners whose game has developed from the beginning under the instruction of coach or teacher, will be the recipients of basic stroke-technique teaching. These stroke techniques are a natural progression from the earlier basic skills.

Older beginners may join coaching sessions with a different stroke method. This will change a coach's approach. He must now assess the usefulness of this stroke method, and may conclude that some corrective work is necessary to improve the skills of the player.

Making corrections

Teaching technical skills will not be enough. Coaches must be able to recognize and correct faults in techniques, strategy and tactics, modifying the players' approach to technique, and correcting any mistaken ideas about how skills are performed. Remember any modification, any correction, must allow a beginner to achieve a positive result.

Guidelines for correction

• Correct faults one at a time
• Use a brief explanation but a sound demonstration
• Make all the corrections progressively
• Remember that the tactical objective is just as important as the technical work
• Work the corrections into play situations.

These five fundamentals are your guide to assessing error and making corrections.

Forehand Drive

Individual interpretation is an important factor in how a young player will develop his strokeplay, and the major influence will be the grip. See the illustrations of the stroke played with the basic Eastern grip (opposite) and Western grip (page 56). Note that the player using a Western grip has a stance that is more open and closer to the ball - these characteristics add up to a very good forehand player with heavy topspin.

A player could have a variation of grips anywhere between Eastern and Western grip. A coach must remember that if the Western grip is favoured by a young player, the ball will be a little closer to the body and the stance more open, but if there is any doubt in a player's mind as to which grip to use, stick with the basic Eastern as it is the simpler method to teach.

Forehand Drive - using Eastern grip
1. The preparation
2. The transitional phase from backswing to forward swing
3. The point of impact
4. The follow-through

Eastern grip
Stroke Method
1. Start from the position of readiness.
2. Take the racket back early.
3. Make a smooth connection between the backswing and forward swing.
4. Prepare on the right foot; step in with the left foot.
5. Hit through the ball, striking it when it is about level with the leading hip, at a comfortable distance from the body and at a comfortable height.
6. On completion of the stroke, the racket finishes at least at head height and the upper body finishes facing the net.
7. Maintain balance.
8. Return to a position of readiness.

Coaching points

• Palm behind the handle. This is a natural extension of the hand.
• The maximum strength is achieved this way.
• Easy to hit effectively balls of varying height.
• Lends itself easily to variations of spin.

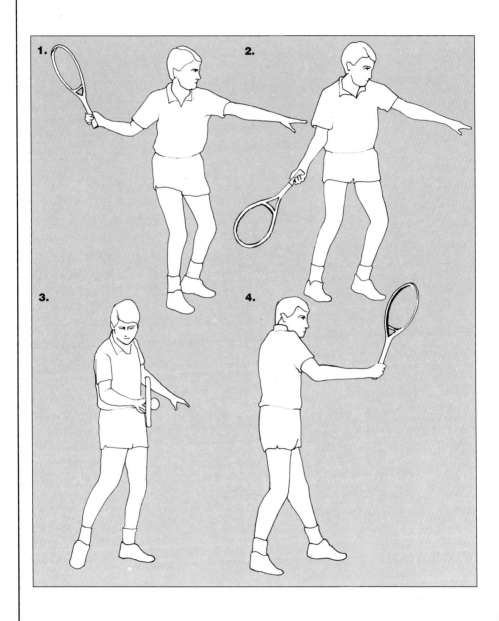

Forehand Drive - using Western grip
1. The preparation
2. The transition phase from backswing to forward swing
3. The point of impact
4. The follow-through

Western grip

Points
- Palm under the handle.
- Natural position of the hand for hitting balls above waist height.
- Makes for hitting stronger shots on high balls.
- Encourages the use of more topspin.

Stroke method
1. Start from the position of readiness.
2. Take the racket back early.
3. Make a smooth connection between backswing and forward swing. (The loop may tend to be more extravagant.)
4. Prepare on the right foot, keeping the stance open with the body weight forward at impact.
5. Hit through the ball, striking it when it is about level with the leading hip, at a comfortable distance from the body and at a comfortable height.
6. At impact the arm should be less extended and the ball should be played closer to the body than in the Eastern forehand grip.
7. Controlled wrist action is essential because of the closed racket face.
8. On completion of the stroke, the racket finishes level with the head and the upper body finishes facing the net.

Single-handed Backhand Drive

The grip is obtained by taking an Eastern forehand grip and then moving the hand inwards a quarter of a turn, with the thumb diagonally across the back of the handle. The hand is now more on top of the racket.

Single-handed Backhand Drive
1. The preparation
2. The transitional phase from backswing to forward swing
3. The point of impact
4. The follow-through

Points
1. Greater strength behind the handle achieved with this grip.
2. Grip gives greater flexibility, encouraging a variety of shots.
3. A sensitive as well as a strong grip.
4. Encourages all-round racket face control.

Stroke method
1. Start from the position of readiness (grip with Eastern forehand grip).
2. Take the racket back early.
3. Change the grip as the body turns away. More body turn is required than for a forehand drive. The back of the hitting shoulder is towards the net at the end of the back swing.
4. Make a smooth connection between backswing and forward swing (shallow loop) using the freehand to support the racket at the throat during the backswing.
5. Prepare on the left leg, step in and across with the right leg, putting the foot into position before the ball is struck. Keep the knees bent.
6. Hit through the ball when it is slightly in front of the leading hip at a comfortable distance away from the body.
7. Develop lift in the forward swing, swing from low to high.
8. Racket finishes around head height with the upper body facing the net at the completion of the stroke.
9. Maintain balance throughout the shot.

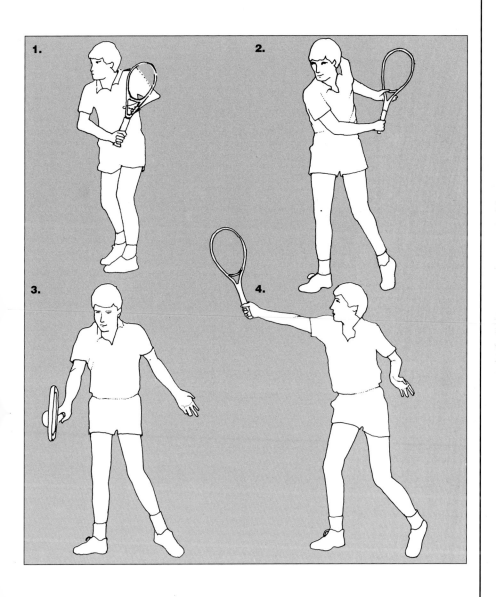

BASIC STROKE TECHNIQUES

Two-handed Backhand Drive

Grip

The right hand takes a single-handed backhand grip. The left hand takes an Eastern forehand grip. The hands should be close together.

Points

• Increased strength using two hands.
• Increased racket-face control with two hands.
• Possible extra power and speed of the swing.
• Increased flexibility and disguise on shots.

Stroke method

1. This stroke derives its effectiveness from the two sound grips.
2. Early preparation is important because both hands must be brought together on the racket handle in good time to play a shot.
3. A player needs to get closer to the ball because of the restricted reach.
4. Less shoulder-turn prior to the shot as with the single-handed backhand.
5. Important to step forward into the shot. Prepare on the left foot and step into the shot on the right foot.
6. There are two basic methods of playing this stroke - keeping two hands on the racket throughout the stroke; and releasing with the top hand after making contact with the ball.
7. There are many successful variations of this stroke.

Some players try to avoid using their backhand by running round it and playing the shot on the forehand - most players' stronger side. The result is that competence on the backhand side is slow to develop because of the lack of practice, and they are left with a weakness in their game. Coaches must ensure that young players keep practising their backhand.

For many young players the question is whether they should use a backhand with one hand or two. If there is some doubt a coach must study the advantages and disadvantages of both and encourage young players to experiment until they are sure which stroke they wish to use. Once the decision is made, they should stick to it and make it as effective and reliable as possible.

Lobs

Forehand and backhand lobs are groundstrokes and should closely follow the swing pattern of basic forehand and backhand drives. The grips are the same as for forehand and backhand drives.

Points

- This stroke has strong defensive qualities.
- This stroke is used to break up the play of a strong net player.
- Played well, the lob can turn defence into attack.

Stroke method

1. Prepare the backswing early.
2. Keep racket head well below the height of the ball.
3. Make lifting action steep - very low to very high.
4. Keep a smooth, slow, controlled swing.
5. The racket face must be slightly open at impact.
6. Keep the wrist firm at impact.
7. Finish with a high follow through.
8. Maintain balance.

Backhand Lob
1. The preparation
2. The transitional phase between backswing and forward swing
3. The point of impact
4. The follow-through

Service

The service is a crucial stroke in the game. Getting off to a good start generates confidence in the player and this is very important for the rest of the player's game.

Developing a sound service technique is at the heart of developing a good service. The strength of a player's serving ability will depend on all-round safe methods for first and second services.

There is more individual interpretation of the service than almost any other stroke in the game but this does not affect the fact that good serving is based on sound basics. Keep the action simple, place the ball in the air with one hand, throw the racket face at it with the other.

The service grip
This grip is between the two basic grips of Eastern forehand and backhand and is called the chopper grip. Very young players may find it easier at the beginning to use the forehand grip and adjust later as skill improves. The advantages of the chopper grip are:
• It gives more flexibility
• It encourages greater racket-head speed
• It lends itself to the development of controlled spin
• It allows more opportunity for variations.

Stroke method
1. Take a sideways stance with the feet roughly shoulder-width apart. Be comfortable but maintain a strong throwing stance: a position of readiness for service.
2. Look directly at the target.
3. The ball and the racket hands start together to produce a rhythmical beginning.
4. Place the ball accurately in the air just above full hitting height and slightly in front of the body.
5. The racket should be in an explosive throwing position behind the head before the hit takes place.
6. Stretch upwards for maximum hitting height.
7. Body weight follows the same direction as the ball.
8. Retain balance throughout the action.

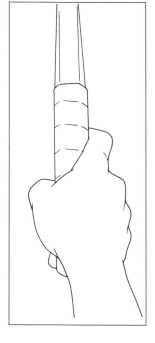

Above: Chopper (service) grip
Right: The service

Volleys

Before making a study of the technique involved, it is worth considering some interesting points.

The distance between the volleyer and the baseline player is very much reduced. This means there is less time to operate the volley. A player must be more alert and use a ready position from which movements can be quick in reaching the ball.

There is now only one flight of the ball to contend with, so quick thinking and quick reactions are essential in assessing the changing height of the ball during this one flight.

Grip

The grips for volley are the same as those used for groundstroke play. Initially this means a change of grip between forehand and backhand. This method of gripping may change as skills and confidence begin to work together. Refining the grips now becomes more personal and the usual reason for change is the desire to create greater flexibility. There should, however, be no great hurry to move away from the basic grips.

Method

1. Start from the position of readiness.
2. Keep the backswing of the racket short.
3. Play the volley at the side and slightly in front (sound hitting area to contact point).
4. Emphasize the racket-head punching the ball.
5. Use the racket-head correctly.
6. Keep a firm grip of the racket to control the action of the volley.
7. Keep the follow-through short.
8. Maintain balance, get the weight behind the shot.
9. Make a quick recovery.

Volleys
Top: Single-handed backhand volley
1. Ready position
2. Point of impact
3. Follow-through
Bottom: Forehand volley
1. Preparation
2. Point of impact
3. Follow-through

1. **2.** **3.**

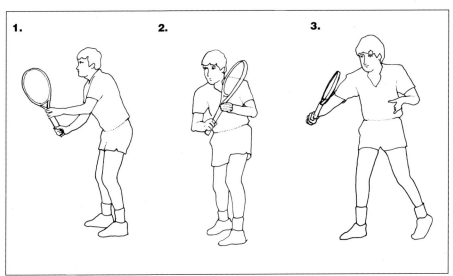

1. **2.** **3.**

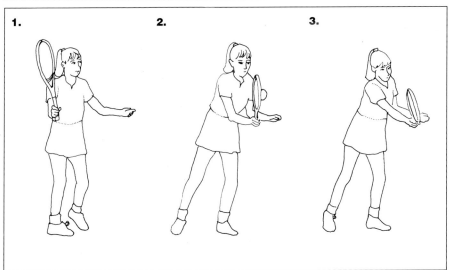

Smash

Playing from the front of the court will never be secure until a player can master the most thrilling shot in the game - the smash. It is probably the most under-practised stroke of amateur tennis.

Usually the player has to move backwards from the net position to get into a sound hitting position. It is difficult to move backwards quickly and remain poised and well balanced. A sideways movement is often the answer.

The smash is an extension of the service except that your opponent has placed the ball in the air for you (badly unfortunately). You must correct this by good movement to align the ball for a good smash.

Grip

The chopper grip should be used (see Service), although in the early stages of learning many young children find it more comfortable to play with the easier grip, the forehand grip. This will be readjusted as skill and confidence grow.

Method

1. Move back from the volley position in sideways steps as soon as the lob is identified.
2. Take the racket back into a throwing position early using a shortened backswing.
3. Take a longer last stride just before throwing the racket head at the ball, using the non-hitting hand to assist correct alignment to the ball (sound hitting area and contact point).
4. Get the body weight into the smash and hit at full stretch.
5. Recover to a ready position.

Summary

The reason for coaching basic strokeplay is to give the majority of beginners a sound foundation for development. Basic strokes are simple in their construction and the grips used are close to one another thus making the earlier stages of learning to play easier. All the strokes are played with a minimum of spin on the ball. As skill and confidence grow, changes will occur. Adding spin on the ball will give greater variety and increase tactical options in matches.

Teachers and coaches should appreciate that within any class of young players some will hit the ball better than others mainly because they have better coordination, a better feeling for the racket work and seem more able to play rallies than normal. Even so their technique should be studied and corrections should be made to keep them close to the basic form. This way they will gain more from their immediate advantages than others in the class and have the opportunity to develop into even better players.

These young players and the average adult player usually show quite distinctive common errors within the stroke framework and it is worth a little time and effort to make corrections with the use of teaching aids.

COMMON ERRORS AND TEACHING AIDS

Common Errors and Teaching Aids

Positioning

The common error of getting too close to the ball with the elbow tucked in close to the body cramps the swing and tends to make the racket head drop.

Correction with teaching aid: Use the palm of the racket hand, swing with hand, strike and follow-through (use a soft ball) then introduce the racket using the tram lines to help groove ball sense.

Forehand drive

1. A common error is to cramp the swing as a result of crossing the arms.

Correction with teaching aid: Encourage rotation of the top half of the body. The striking hand is behind the back.

2. Another is a poor follow-through, with a bent arm and a strangling effect at the end of the swing.

Correction with teaching aid: Racket shaft meets non-hitting hand high and towards target.

Backhand drive

1. A common error is failure to support the racket when it is taken back. This leads to a loss of control of the swing and racket face which makes the shot directionless.

Correction with teaching aid: Instruct the player to use the non-hitting hand to support the take-back and leave hand on for a little way into the forward swing.

2. Another is the use of a pushing action, rather than a swing. The body is usually too close, or behind the ball, and the racket head down.

Correction with teaching aid: Check application of ball sense, make the player swing with the back of the hand, strike and follow through (use sponge ball) before introducing the racket.

Correction with teaching aid: Bounce the ball on a bench top and when the racket is travelling to strike it, the racket head will naturally be up to start with. Strike and follow through. An equally effective teaching aid is to kneel on the ground doing the same movement.

Serving

1. The ball is hit too low, with the arm bent and the knees collapsing. This results in poor placement of the ball.

Correction with teaching aid: As the coach, take over the placement of the ball. Give plenty of verbal encouragement to make the player hit the ball at the highest reaching point.

Correction with teaching aid: Use the simple method. Place the ball in the air and let it fall back into the same hand keeping the hand high. If you have a stringless racket, use this for further exercise.

2. There is a general lack of rhythm and coordination.

Usually a player takes the racket back too far before placing the ball, or the ball is placed too early before the racket moves. Young children particularly may have difficulty in separating their hands which leads to jerky racket work and poor placement of the ball.

Correction with teaching aid: Replace racket with extra ball and with both hands (arms) working rhythmically, throw the extra ball at the ball placed in the air.

Correction with teaching aid: As the coach, control the movement of the racket hand and even take over the placement of the ball.

3. Moving the front foot and foot faulting.

Correction with teaching aid: Place racket handle on front foot then serve. The racket handle will stop the player stepping forward.

4. Hips come forward too early, with the right foot kicking through before contact is made with the ball.

Correction with teaching aid: Place a racket handle on the near foot, then serve. Don't worry if the racket handle topples off after impact. It is possible to put a racket handle on both feet. These give a clear picture of how and when the transfer of weight is made.

5. After the introduction of the chopper grip, failure to get the racket face square on the ball.

Correction with teaching aid: Shadow serving against stop netting will demonstrate the need to push the wrist outward to square the racket face.

6. Follow-through past the wrong side of the body.

Correction with teaching aid: Place boxes on the court at the correct side so, if the follow-through is correct, they are hit by the player.

Volleying

Excessive backswing of the racket head.

Correction with teaching aid: A simple but very effective method is to ask the player to first catch the ball with his racket hand then hit it in exactly the same way with the racket.

Smashing

Square to the net and staggering back to position under the ball.

Correction with teaching aid: Ask the player to move forwards and backwards in a sideways position using the non-hitting hand to guide the ball into the correct hitting position. The ball should be caught, the player should check his position and then do the same using his racket.

Summary

Correcting the common faults is important in all strokeplay and, by making sensible use of teaching aids, sessions of correction can be made interesting and enjoyable as well as very rewarding for coach and player. Even in class work, teaching aids are invaluable for making sessions enjoyable while working at developing sound techniques.

PLAYING WITH SPIN

Playing with Spin

Whatever has been said in previous chapters about basic skills and basic strokes, beginners will put spin on the ball, and for the majority putting spin on the ball will have been unintentional. Those in opposition to shots with spin will certainly have experienced how disconcerting it can be to play a shot against a ball that is spinning severely.

• It upsets the footwork when a player thinks he has positioned well.

• It upsets the rhythm of the swing.

• It upsets a player's timing, causing possible mishitting of shots.

• If the player can intentionally spin well and vary it over the shots, it can upset his opponent's method of playing and cause all sorts of anxieties.

Many young players will question the oddities of the bounce of the ball caused by spin so it is important that teachers and coaches understand what happens when spin is put on the ball and how one should cope with it.

Playing with spin can be very stimulating to beginners, and sessions with them on how spin works will add interest and enjoyment to the learning of racket skills. The coach must develop his own skills with spin to demonstrate clearly how to assess spin on the ball and the countermeasures to take when playing against spin.

Sidespin (opposite)
Left: Backhand sidespin
Right: Forehand sidespin
Different types of spin (below)
1. Flat/lifted
2. Slice
3. Topspin

Types of Spin

Topspin
An in-flight ball which spins forwards has been hit with topspin.
Topspin alters the behaviour of the ball. Before the bounce the ball tends to drop quickly. After the bounce it travels upwards quickly with a fairly high bounce.

Slice
An in-flight ball which spins backwards has been hit with slice. Slice alters the behaviour of the ball, making it stay in the air for longer. It bounces more slowly and has less forward momentum.

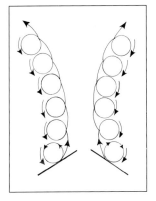

A ball played with slice also skids.

Sidespin

Topspin and slice can be further complicated by sidespin. When play with sidespin and sliced the ball moves through the air sideways and forwards. After bouncing it continues to move sideways and forwards.

Coaches should encourage young players to experiment with hitting the ball on different trajectories, increasing or decreasing the amount of spin until they become accustomed to the altered behaviour of the flight and bounce of the ball.

After a little practice (which can be done simply by dropping and hitting a series of balls over the net with suggested spins), they will begin to realize how the head and face of the racket must be in control to create the spins effectively. However, the fundamentals of strokeplay still apply.

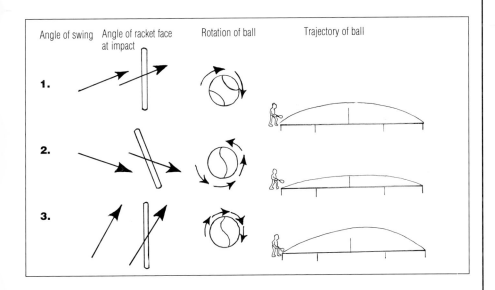

Angle of swing	Angle of racket face at impact	Rotation of ball	Trajectory of ball
1.			
2.			
3.			

Forehand Drive

Topspin (using the Eastern grip)

Technical points

- Maintain a firm grip on the racket.
- Make earlier preparation than normal.
- Begin with normal backswing.
- Before beginning the forward swing the racket head should be much lower than the striking height of the ball.
- Use hand brushing action up and forwards against the back of the ball.
- Keep racket face vertical to the ground at impact.
- Control wrist action after the hit to encourage racket head speed.
- Keep racket face closed during the follow-through.
- Body weight should follow through upwards and forwards.
- Maintain balance throughout.

Tactical value

- It allows more margin for error when hitting aggressively or defensively from any part of the court.
- It gives a higher trajectory over the net.
- It creates a higher bounce causing problems for an opponent.
- It makes the ball drop quickly at the feet of a volleyer.
- It allows increased angles to be played.
- It is useful for counter-attack and for a change of pace.

Forehand Drive with topspin (below)
1. Racket head lowered ready for forward swing
2. Point of impact
3. Follow-through

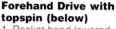

1. 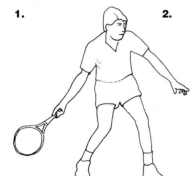 **2.**  **3.**

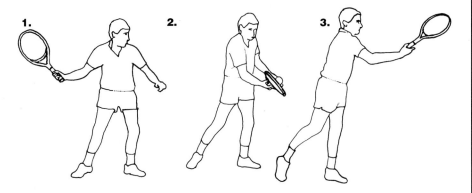

1. 2. 3.

Forehand Drive with slice (above)
1. Backswing
2. Point of impact
3. Follow-through

Slice (using the Eastern Grip)

Technical points
- Use basic forehand grip.
- Use normal backswing.
- Before beginning the forward swing, keep racket head well above the striking height of the ball.
- Hit down and through the ball with the racket face slightly open.
- Make firm contact under the back of the ball.
- Keep the wrist firm and the weight of the body travelling in the direction of the shot.
- Feel that you are holding the ball on the strings longer than when playing a basic drive.
- On the follow-through the face of the racket must remain open.
- Maintain good balance.

Tactical value
- The slice is good for sound defensive play under pressure of speed of shot, height, width and length of ball.
- The lower bounce created by slice is difficult for the opponent to play.
- Useful for playing approach shots when attacking the net.
- Adds accuracy to placement of the ball in opponent's half of the court.
- Gives better control in windy conditions and on courts that are slow and greasy after rain.
- Lends itself to changing the flight and pace of the ball.

Backhand Drive

Topspin using basic backhand grip

Technical points
- Use basic backhand grip.
- Prepare earlier than for normal backhand drive.
- Use normal backswing with racket head very much lower than the height of the ball at the end of the backswing.
- On the forward swing, the racket head brushes up the back of the ball driving up and forwards.
- Racket face is vertical to the ground at impact.
- Controlled wrist action over the back of the ball will encourage overspin towards the chosen target area. Racket face closes during the follow-through.
- Body weight follows through upwards and forwards.
- Maintain balance throughout the stroke.

Tactical value
- Allows for more margin of error when hitting aggressively or defensively from any part of the court with a higher trajectory over the net.
- The higher bounce with topspin may cause problems for an opponent.
- The topspin causes the ball to dip quickly to the feet of a volleyer.
- Allows increased angles to be played.
- Useful for counter-attacking play and changing the pace of the ball. In this way it can break an opponent's rhythm.

Two-handed topspin

The points given for the single-handed backhand apply in two-handed play. Two-handed players using topspin do have the ability to achieve incredible angles. When playing with increased topspin, these players drop the head of the racket much more than the single-handed player, chiefly because of a more flexible use of the wrist of the bottom hand.

Backhand Drive
Top: Two-handed with topspin
1. Backswing
2. Point of impact
3. Follow-through
Bottom: With topspin
1. Backswing
2. Point of impact
3. Follow-through

1.   **2.**   **3.**

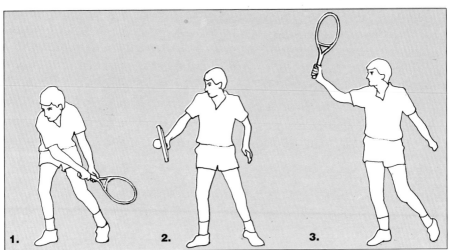

1.   **2.**   **3.**

Backhand Drive with slice
1. Backswing
2. Point of impact
3. Follow-through

Slice using basic backhand grip
Technical points
• Use normal backswing.
• On the forward swing, the racket head starts from a point much higher than the striking height of the ball.
• Hit down and forward through the ball with the racket face slightly open.
• Make a firm impact down and under the ball.
• Keep the wrist firm and the weight of the body going into the shot.
• Feel the ball on the strings of the racket longer than for the normal backhand.
• Throughout the follow-through the face of the racket remains open.
• Body weight follows direction of the ball. Maintain balance throughout the stroke.

1.   **2.**   **3.**

Tactical value
- Good for defensive play when under pressure from the height, width and length of the ball.
- Slice keeps the ball low and this may cause problems for an opponent.
- Slice is useful for playing approach shots when attacking the net.
- Assists accuracy and placement of the ball.
- Allows for better control of the ball in windy conditions and is very effective on slow, damp courts.
- Lends itself to delicate angled shots.

Two-handed slice

Two-handed players will follow closely the same points as for the single-handed player. Those players, however, who keep both hands on the racket when playing with slice appear to play less fluently than those who release the top hand after impact. Therefore it is not surprising that in recent years many of the top two-handed players have been playing more and more with one hand when defending under pressure with slice. If the grips are sound initially it is worth cultivating a single-handed slice. Coaches must choose the appropriate time to introduce this to young players.

Service Spins

The earlier introduction of spin on the service will aid overall security. It develops a sound aggressive second service and can help to eliminate many double faults. This in turn increases confidence, allowing a player to serve first balls more convincingly.

Although the principles of putting spin on the ball are the same, hitting with spin from above your head will give a completely different feeling because the swing of the racket is now:
• On a different plane from forehand and backhand;
• Making contact with the ball in a different area;
• Bringing in regular sidespin.

It was earlier suggested that young players find the chopper grip difficult to handle early on in the learning process so, once again, let the young player begin with a basic forehand grip and concentrate on developing a slice service. Encourage the young player to get to a chopper grip as confidence grows because later on you will want to introduce the topspin service to them and this service needs the chopper grip to be wholly successful.

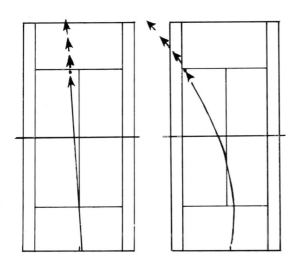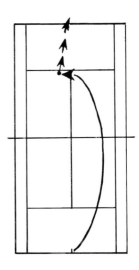

Slice service using the chopper grip

Top far left: Flat service
Top left: Slice service
Above: Topspin service

Technical points
• Placement of the ball is slightly further to the right of the body.
• Racket-face is in a semi-closed position at impact.
• Racket-face continues its movement round the outside of the ball, making contact with the ball on the top right-hand side - hitting from left to right.
• Always maintain a strong throwing action.
• Imagine holding the ball on the strings longer than for a basic service.
• Always have a good follow-through.
• Maintain good balance.

Tactical value
• Takes an opponent wide of the court, because the ball swings with slice.
• Forces an opponent to play too close and too far away from the body, making it difficult to get the correct hitting area and contact point.
• Useful for deceiving an opponent with speed and with a different flight of the ball.
• The slice service keeps the ball low after the bounce.

Topspin service using the chopper grip

Technical points

• Placement of the ball on the left side of the body and slightly less forward than for the basic service.
• The ball placement will not be so high.
• The back should be arched.
• Upwards brushing action of the racket face up and across the ball.
• Maintain a strong throwing action.
• Good wrist action to take the racket face up and across the ball.
• Imagine the racket face turning over the top of the ball after impact.
• Body weight follows the direction of the ball upwards and forwards.
• Maintain good balance.

Tactical value

• Allows for margin of error (greater net clearance).
• A higher, sharper bounce occurs with topspin causing problems for an opponent.
• Adds greater confidence to serving in general.
• Higher trajectory of ball over net can give a volleyer behind the service more time to reach a good court position.

 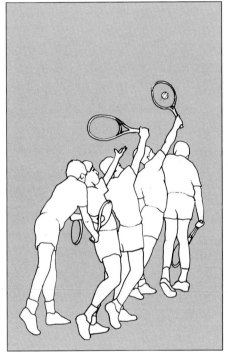

Above left: The slice service
Above right: The topspin service

Summary

Remember that every ball hit will have spin and when a player can intentionally apply spin in the different ways suggested, he will be able to confuse an opponent and make his hitting ability less effective.

Encourage players to appreciate that there must always be a good reason for playing a shot with spin. Just putting spin on the ball is not good enough. It does broaden a player's tactical options and adds quality of play. It is a fascinating art, and a coach and his young players can have many enjoyable sessions developing spin skills.

Now would be a good time to get your senior players back to demonstrate the techniques for your beginners. Show how spin plays a major part in the development of the game.

Your beginners will love trying to play with spin, so let them enjoy experimenting with it. Encourage them and stimulate their interest in learning how to play well with the new-found skill.

TEACHING AND DEVELOPING BASIC TACTICS

Teaching and Developing Basic Tactics

Before players are able to develop basic tactics it is important to know (a) what are considered to be basic tactics and (b) how they can be used at different levels of performance within the tennis court dimensions.

These basic tactics are the foundation for all levels of play but they also appear to be different when top players put them into action. The reason for this is their more sophisticated strokeplay and greater variety of strokes. When watching these top players, one becomes so excited about their wonderful hitting when manoeuvring fast around the court that one fails to watch the tactical way in which the shots are being used. If a coach can arrange a video session of a match (and they are available),and study it closely with his group of players, all the basic tactics can be seen. At the same time the coach can feed to them the important points.

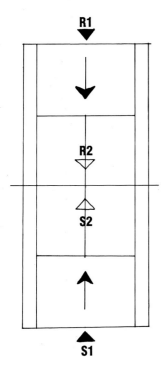

The Singles Game

Basic court positions

Service and return

The server is positioned behind the baseline near the centre mark (S1) while the receiver of the serve is positioned just outside the baseline, covering both sides of the service equally (R1).

The server may change his position for serving to create a different line of attack (S2). It is important that the receiver adjusts his position to counter this change (R2).

Rallying positions

The server and the receiver, having exchanged the first two shots played (serve and return), will now position themselves three or four feet behind their own baseline near the centre mark (S1 and R1). They will adjust their positions to take account of the varying angles and depth of shots played, and always return to a near-central position after hitting the ball. Should players move forward from these rallying positions to develop net play, seven to eight feet from the net is a sound basic volleying position.

Once a rally is under way, court positions are never fixed and they must always reflect the pattern of play that is developing.

Singles game - playing positions, baseline and volleys

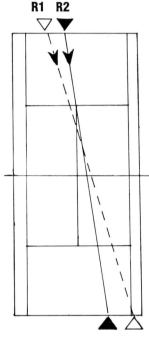

R1   R2

S1   S2

Singles game - serve and
return positions

Basic tactics

• Retain good positions on court. The better a player's position related to the play, the easier it is to move into a good hitting position with a better execution of the stroke required.
• Put and keep the ball in play, and play accurately to achieve a tactical plan.
• Make the opponent run. This puts a strain on ball sense, judgement and timing.
• Exploit a weakness.
• Wrong foot an opponent. This is the beginning of the art of not playing the obvious shot.
• Know your own strengths and weaknesses. The sounder a player's technical ability, the more chance he will have of following a tactical plan.
• Be patient and don't rush to make the winning shot.
• Develop play from sound planning.

Good positioning

Players appreciate the need to be alert and ready, moving quickly to retrieve an opponent's shot, but many fail to use the same quick movements to recover to a good ready position in relation to the play. Players must learn to respond to their own good shots and position accordingly. Many tactical opportunities can be lost if they don't.

Never forget basic position.

Putting and keeping the ball in play

Players should be encouraged to hit the ball to a consistent length. In this way a player can keep an opponent behind the baseline where he will find it difficult to hit a winning shot.

Players must realize that it is not only winners that bring good results. Most matches are lost by players making too many errors. The more times a player returns the ball over the net and into play the more an opponent is likely to make mistakes. Good players develop a balance between consistency and aggression.

- **Make your opponent run**

In this way a player never allows an opponent to settle down. There is less time for him to play his shots and the continual changing of position on court breaks the rhythm of his strokeplay. Remember that players enjoy hitting from fixed positions because it is easier to keep a grooved series of strokes. Never allow an opponent this luxury.

- **Exploit a weakness**

Right from the beginning of a match when opponents are knocking up, they should be assessing one another's play and searching for weaknesses they can exploit. Having discovered a weakness, they will remember it and work out a way of using it to their advantage. Each will try not to give the game away. They will keep the opponent guessing as to when the weakness will be attacked.

- **Wrong foot your opponent**

This is the most satisfying of tactical moves. It is linked strongly with making an opponent run from side to side. The rhythm of this side-to-side movement will lull an opponent into over-anticipating the next ball and move too early, allowing the striker to play the ball back into the same area twice in succession. This tactic works well against a quick mover about the court. Slower players do not move out of the corners quickly enough, and may be waiting for the wrong-footing shot.

Strengths and weaknesses

These are all part of a player's make-up and each individual player should understand his own game. In this way players will use their abilities much more intelligently doing what they do best and not taking unnecessary risks in areas where they know they have difficulties. They should be patient and wait for better opportunities. If in doubt, players should use their most reliable shot.

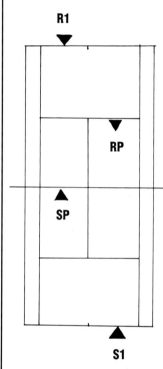

Doubles game - serving positions

The Doubles Game

Many players find this game much more attractive to play. They feel more relaxed and enjoy the shared responsibility. Indeed there usually seems to be more fun when playing doubles.

Playing a good doubles game still depends on good basic tactics but those who enjoy the doubles game must remember they are part of a team and the strengths and weaknesses of both players must be part of their success together.

Basic court positions

• **Starting positions**
The server is positioned behind the baseline a little wider of the centre mark than for singles. The serving partner (SP) is positioned close to the net, about halfway between the outside sideline and the centre service line. The receiver is in the same position as in singles. The receiving partner (RP) is positioned just inside the left-hand service box at an equal distance between the inside sideline and the centre service line.

• **Playing positions**
Players will change their positions to develop possible winning situations. The server may move from baseline to mid-court (S2) and then get into a good volleying position (S3) joining his partner for a strong attacking position. The positions of the receiver and his partner will be controlled by how good a return of serve the receiver can play. The receiver will hold his position after returning the ball, while his partner may move forwards slightly and retreat to a defensive position alongside his partner (RP3). The receiver may follow a good return to the net (R2) and join his partner (RP2) in a balanced counter-attacking position. The server's partner (SP3), if lobbed, may join his partner (S1) on the baselines to develop strong defensive play.

Basic tactics

• Retain good positions on court. The better the team's position on court related to the play, the easier it is to execute the strokes.
• Remember this is a team game so all tactics are a shared operation.

THE DOUBLES GAME

• Doubles is a more volleying game so get nearer to the net quickly before your opponents. This gives you the opportunity to hit shots downwards while the opposition must play upwards over the net.

• Try to keep the ball low over the net. This is very important when returning service.

• The better a team's technical ability, the greater chance there is of keeping the ball in play and following a tactical plan.

• Play accurately to create space. This will give your partner more opportunities to win points at the net.

• Play on the weaker opponent.

• Hold your service game.

• Develop a sound team plan.

Players take a little time to know if they can play well together and that their different strokeplay complements one another. This is very important when playing and enjoying the doubles game.

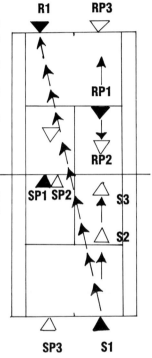

Doubles game - changing positions

95

How to Proceed

• Set up singles and doubles matches within young groups.
• Try to pair them off with equal ability.
• Use the short tennis game early on and then use the low-compression ball on the full court.
• Use a shortened scoring method to circulate the players around from singles to doubles.
• Concentrate on court positions, rallying and recovery.
• Do not push the technical areas too hard in this early tactical session.

In this way the coach can watch over his beginners and assess their individual responses in the early stages of the game. The coach will find it to his advantage to position himself behind each player in turn. In this way it is easy to encourage the player , and by following the flight of the ball as if the coach was playing himself, he can judge his young player's approach to positioning and recovery. A little advice while the player is working will help him to appreciate this important area of play.

In the doubles game follow the same procedure. Stay behind each player advising on correct movement as each ball is played. Encourage the server and receiver to move to the net. Stand alongside the server, move forward as the player serves, getting him to move forward as well when he steadies the forward movement to volley. The young player does the same and plays the volley. The coach moves forward again into a good volleying position at the net. Again the player follows the coach's movements. Repeat the same exercise with the receiver.

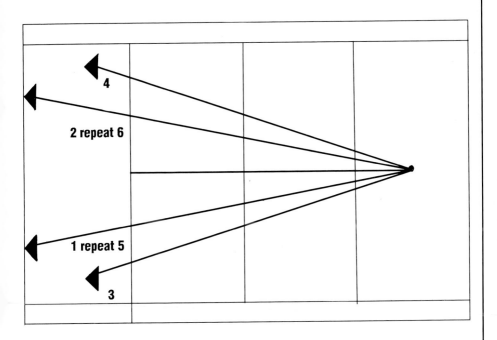

Developing the tactical game

Rallying with 6 balls.

Use a low compression ball throughout this session.

• **Return of service**

The coach should position the player correctly and then serve gentle balls from his own service line. Serve to the right court first, one ball to the forehand and another to the backhand. Then repeat the same exercise to the left court.

• **Rallying position**

The coach should use a six-ball feeding sequence. With the young player in a ready position to the centre and just behind the baseline, feed the first ball to the forehand side. The player should move, play the ball and recover to the centre.

Feed the second ball to the backhand side. The player should move, play the ball then recover to the centre.

Feed the third ball to the forehand but a little shorter,

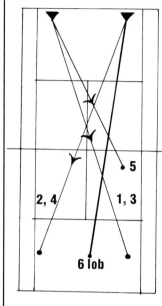

2, 4

1, 3

5

6 lob

Making the opponent run

encouraging forward and sideways movement. The player should move, hit the ball and recover to the centre.

Feed the fourth ball to the same area of the court on the backhand side. The player should move, hit the ball and recover once more.

Fifth and sixth balls are a repeat of the first two balls. Take each of your players through the same sequence; use some of the group to ball-boy while waiting to play.

• Putting and keeping the ball in play

With six players on a court in three pairs, start the sequence. The first pair on court rallies within the singles court. They count the number of shots played until play breaks down. They play three rallies then total the number of shots played. This total will be the target for the second and third pairs to try and beat.

The second practice has three players playing against the other three. The first player of each team play the first two shots, the second players of the team plays the third and fourth shots, and, finally, the third players play shots five and six. They should aim to make a continuous rally and then repeat the playing sequence until play breaks down. Now, instead of rallying, they should play for points.

The three-against-three format can be used for team rallying, with teams of six on each court in competition with other teams. Remember that the players must stay in strict rotation in each of the exercises.

• Make your opponent run

With the coach playing the role of running opponent, your younger players will especially enjoy this exercise. Using a six-ball sequence, the player bounces a ball and hits it cross-court from his forehand side. The coach runs to hit the ball. Now the young player moves across to the backhand side of the court, bounces another ball and plays a backhand cross-court for the coach to run for again. The third and fourth balls are repeats of the first two, the coach moving from one side of the court to the other. The fifth ball played by the young player is hit short and gently into the opposite service box (the coach runs forwards) and the player hits the sixth ball over the coach's head. (Coach now chases back towards the baseline to retrieve the ball.) End of sequence.

Beginners find it difficult to hold six balls, so they should use a partner to hand them the ball to hit. This should be done as quickly as possible between them to keep the coach running. The coach playing the role of a struggling opponent will give a clear picture of how to make an opponent run. The coach can now relax and encourage his young players to try these shots to make one another run around the court.

• **Wrong-foot your opponent**

Again the coach should play the role of the opponent, using the same method of hitting as in the exercise for making an opponent run. Again the young player bounces a ball and hits it cross-court from the forehand side and plays another cross-court ball but from the backhand side. The next two balls are a repeat of the first two, by which time the coach should be running from one side of the court to the other. The fifth ball is now played back in the same direction as the last ball played. The coach, anticipating another cross-court ball, moves quickly and is wrong-footed. Remember the young player will need his partner to hand him the ball each time.

Conclusions

Simple feeding methods, hitting from the bounced ball, will give a clear picture of how to make these basic tactics work. Now the players can go on court and try to play these tactics. They will probably have enjoyed the coach's willingness to be an Aunt Sally and will respond accordingly in other sessions.

PLANNING LESSONS AND PROGRAMMES

Planning Lessons and Programmes

Whatever technical knowledge and teaching ability a coach may have, success in coaching players will only be achieved by fitting all the skill factors into a well-planned programme. Planning lessons requires constant evaluation of the players' mental and physical skills in an attempt to understand their coaching needs. In this way the coach can set individual goals of achievement that are within their capabilities, and enable a player to work on them while you are working with others.

Planning Lessons

Individual lessons give a young player exclusive use of the coach, but private lessons can be far more expensive than taking lessons with a group of players. These individual lessons also deny the player a means of measuring his skills and progress against other players of similar ability.

Group coaching also has problems, as players do not get as much individual attention. Space may also be a limiting factor, particularly if the groups are large. Any beginner who can have both individual coaching and coaching within a group gains in every way. The coach should strive to give everyone the same benefits if possible. To do this a coach must arrange to have assistant coaches working with him. But whether it is an individual or group coaching session, its success depends on common factors.

In a session:
• The players must feel they know you, so introduce yourself, make them feel comfortable and relaxed and explain the lesson plan.
• Remember the players' names.
• Demonstrate early on in a lesson, slowly and always in good form. Position players correctly so that they can see the points you are stressing. Change these positions for them to see the action from a different angle.

• Give clear instructions so that you can be heard.
• Work to recognize faults and correct, them one at a time. Have no doubts that what you are saying is correct but be prepared to modify just as positively.
• Make all explanations brief and precise.
• Help the individual within the class without actively disturbing the class.
• You cannot do all the feeding. Demonstrate to the class how to feed and cooperate with a partner.
• You must be part of the class. Move around continually, join in the sessions, take over hitting and feeding. In this way a coach keeps a continuous demonstration going.
• Make sure all the players are safe from injury.
• Teach all the skills with simple progressions.
• Keep all the class active feeding, hitting or ball-boying.
• Keep all the activities well within the players' capabilities - individually and in the class. Don't move along too quickly.
• Lead by example in dress, enthusiasm and attitude, on and off the court.
• Encourage the players to practise between lessons.
• Remember that fun and enjoyment are just as important as learning the skills of the game.
• At the end of each lesson gather the class together and talk about the activities of the lesson. Tell them what you have planned for them during the next lesson.

Further planning

It is important to know how many courts you need to enable your class to work at the skills of the game with movement. Too many players on one court is very restricting and very frustrating for the players, as well as making the safety factor more difficult to control. Eight young players per court is a sensible number. If you use three courts in a row, make the middle court the assembly point for all demonstrations and equipment.

Equipment

Make sure you have everything you need because it is important for the smooth running of a lesson.

• Rackets of different sizes, tennis balls, sponge balls, low-compression balls and hoppers for the balls are needed on each court.

• Targets - hoops of different sizes and footballs for aiming at when serving (knocking the ball out of the square).

• A blackboard is useful for showing the layout of the court with players in various positions and the activities each player will perform. Keep records of points scored in competitive games.

• Video equipment if available. Take film of the class at work, demonstrations and individual players in action. These are especially useful if weather delays play.

• Skipping ropes for each individual and a larger rope for class skipping which could form part of a warm-up session or relaxation from skill practice.

• Your 'lesson planning' will tell you what else you may need.

The lesson plan

It is now up to the coach to formulate a lesson around a span of time. One hour is a basis from which to start, mainly because of the concentration levels of beginners. The coach must break down this one-hour lesson into timed components but must still be prepared to change the plan if things don't go the way you anticipated. A lesson plan should contain the following:

Warm-up - Stretching, running, skipping and
hand ball games ....10-15 mins

Selected skills in practice - Select the drills you will need to
stimulate concentrated work .... 10 mins
Relaxed fun games .... 10 mins
Competitive games built around selected skill practice -
10 mins

One hour goes quickly and a coach may feel that the time spent
on the selected skill practice is too little. Increase the lesson time
by 15 minutes to absorb the time taken up by the warm-up period.
Don't let time rush your actions on court.

Planning Programmes

This needs a great deal of thought and much will depend on where
these programmes take place, whether at schools or in parks
(usually in a recreational programme). See what happens at clubs
and arrange coaching and play. Wherever the venue, a successful
programme will be in the hands of the coach. His enthusiasm,
ideas and sheer hard work will be an important factor. It is also
certain that the coach will need other enthusiasts around him to
support his programme.

Considerations

• Court space for coaching against court space for playing time,
particularly in the club environment.
• The length of the programme, not less than six sessions.
• Plan tournaments for everyone, adults and juniors; also family
tournaments.
• Round-robin tournaments with handicapping are enjoyable and
could increase participation.
• Priority of doubles play in the club situation.

Summary

Planning lessons and programmes is governed by the facilities that are available. Court space is so important to a coach. He knows that players must be able to move around and enjoy the freedom of running to hit tennis balls. The keenness and enthusiasm of players of all ages - and what they wish to achieve from coaching - will be important points for the coach to consider, plus many other things before he sets out his plan of action. Whatever plan or programme he devises, he must believe that it is to the advantage of young and old to take part, and convince them that working at their game and improving their skills is fun, enjoyable and very rewarding. Sound planning and developing an enjoyable programme are important priorities.

The coach needs all the help he can get in planning sound, enjoyable sessions. Certain specific reading materials will be of great value - particularly in the areas of racket drills and practices related to the different skills of the game , and competitive games for class sessions. The list of books that follow are those selected because of their importance to group coaching, but other book titles can be obtained from Charles Applewhaite, Director of Coaching for the Lawn Tennis Association.

Being Fit to Play

In general most beginners do not experience the hard physical requirements associated with the higher skill-levels of play, but things change very quickly and there will be much puffing and blowing once these young players begin to rally the ball with a partner. Even in the coaching of the basic skills some form of physical preparation is necessary. Therefore it is important to begin fitness education for young players right at the beginning of any coaching programme.

Specific fitness exercises must be selected by the coach and related to his group of players, bearing in mind their age, sex and present physical development. Really hard fitness routines should come towards the end of any tennis lesson. Skill practice after such a session does not work as the players, especially youngsters, will be too tired to work and concentrate on specific tennis skills.

There is also the problem of time. Warm-up routines at the beginning of the lesson and then later a more vigorous physical session would leave very little skill time, so young players should be encouraged to appear at the courts well before the tennis session starts to do their own warm-up routines. It is a self-discipline that most top players have had to learn. Equally, the hard physical routines should be planned after the tennis lesson or in other periods between tennis activities.

Warm-up and fitness exercises
• Begin with jogging.
• Stretching exercises for tennis - trunk rotations; hamstring stretches; arm and shoulder rotations.

More vigorous exercises
• Skipping - individual or group skipping.
• Shuttle runs, chasing a ball etc.
• Running on the spot - knee jumps.
• Simulated tennis movements, shadowing the movements made by the coach.

This is only a short introduction to warm-up and fitness exercises. I recommend Bev Risman's *Fit for Tennis* to help you with your planning of these activities alongside all technical, skill and tactical lessons.

Book List for Coaches and Teachers

LTA *A Guide for the Introduction of Short Tennis for Teachers*

Charles Applewhaite *Short Tennis Exercise and Games Book*

Charles Applewhaite *Exercises and Games for Tennis*

Charles Applewhaite and Bill Moss *The Skills of the Game*

Charles Applewhaite and Sue Rich *The LTA Professional Drills Book*

Vic Braden *Teaching Children the Vic Braden Way*

Bev Risman *Fit for Tennis*

All these titles are available from the LTA Tennis bookshop. There are many others that broaden the game in all its aspects. All are held in the LTA Bookshop.

Useful addresses
The LTA Bookshop
The Coaching Department
The Lawn Tennis Association Trust
Queen's Club
West Kensington
LONDON W14 9EG

Department of Physical Education and Sports Science
University of Technology
Loughborough
Leicestershire LE11 3TU

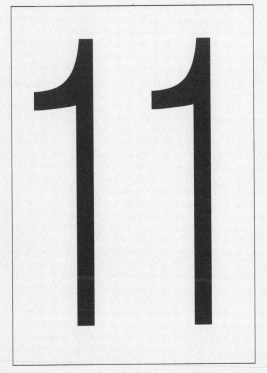

RULES OF TENNIS

RULES OF TENNIS

RULES

Contents

THE SINGLES GAME

1. The Court

The Court shall be a rectangle 78 feet (23.77m.) long and 27 feet (8.23m.) wide.

It shall be divided across the middle by a net suspended from a cord or metal cable of a maximum diameter of one-third of an inch (0.8cm.), the ends of which shall be attached to, or pass over, the tops of the two posts, which shall be not more than 6 inches (15cm.) square or 6 inches (15cm.) in diameter. These posts shall not be higher than 1 inch (2.3cm.) above the top of the net cord. The centres of the posts shall be 3 feet (0.914m.) outside the Court on each side and the height of the posts shall be such that the top of the cord or metal cable shall be 3 feet 6 inches (1.07m.) above the ground.
  When a combined doubles (see Rule 34) and singles Court with a doubles net is used for singles, the net must be supported to a height of 3 feet 6 inches (1.07m.) by means of two posts, called "singles sticks", which shall be not more than 3 inches (7.5cm.) square or 3 inches (7.5cm.) in diameter. The centres of the singles sticks shall be 3 feet (.914m.) outside the singles Court on each side.

The net shall be extended fully so that it fills completely the space between the two posts and shall be of sufficiently small mesh to prevent the ball passing through. The height of the net shall be 3 feet (.914m.) at the centre, where it shall be held down taut by a strap not more than 2 inches (5cm.) wide and completely white in colour. There shall be a band covering the cord or metal cable and the top of the net of not less than 2 inches (5cm.) nor more than 2.5 inches (6.3cm.) in depth on each side and completely white in colour. There shall be no advertisement on the net, strap band or singles sticks. The lines bounding the ends and sides of the Court shall respectively be called the base-lines and the side-lines. On each side of the net, at a distance of 21 feet (6.40m.) from it and parallel with it, shall be drawn the service-lines. The space on each side of the net between the service-line and the side-lines shall be divided into two equal parts called the service-courts by the centre service-line, which must be 2 inches (5cm.) in width, drawn half-way between, and parallel with, the side-line. Each base-line shall be bisected by an imaginary continuation of the centre service-line to a line 4 inches (10cm.) in length and 2 inches (5cm.) in width called "the centre" mark drawn inside the Court, at right angles to and in contact with such base-lines. All other lines shall not be less than 1 inch (2.5cm.) nor more than 2 inches (5cm.) in width, except the base-line, which may be 4 inches (10cm.) in width, and all measurements shall be made to the outside of the lines. All lines shall be of uniform colour. If advertising or any other material is placed at the back of the Court, it may not contain white, or yellow. A light colour may only be used if this does not interfere with the vision of the players.

If advertisements are placed on the chairs of the linesmen sitting at the back of the Court, they may not contain white or yellow. A light colour may only be used if this does not interfere with the vision of the players.

Note: In the case of the *Davis Cup* or other Official Championships of the International Tennis Federation, there shall be a space behind each base-line of not less than 21 feet (6.4m.), and at the sides of not less than 12 feet (3.66m.). The chairs of linesmen may be placed at the back of a court within the 21 feet (6.6m.) or at the side of the court within the 12 feet (3.66m.), provided they do not protrude into that area more than 3 feet (.914m.).

2. Permanent Fixtures

The permanent fixtures of the Court shall include not only the net, posts, singles sticks, cord or metal cable, strap and band, but also, where there are any such, the back and side stops, the stands, fixed or movable seats and chairs round the Court and their occupants, all other fixtures around and above the Court, and the Umpire, Net-cord Judge, Foot-fault Judge, Linesmen and Ball Boys when in their respective places.

Note: For the purpose of this Rule, the word "Umpire" comprehends the Umpire, the persons entitled to a seat on the Court, and all those persons designated to assist the Umpire in the conduct of a match.

RULES OF TENNIS

3. The Ball

The ball shall have a uniform outer surface and shall be white or yellow in colour. If there are any seams they shall be stitchless.

The ball shall be more than two and a half inches (6.35cm) and less than two and five-eighths inches (6.67cm) in diameter, and more than two ounces (56.7 grams) and less than two and one-sixteenth ounces (58.5 grams) in weight.

The ball shall have a bound of more than 53 inches (135cm.) and less than 58 inches (147cm.) when dropped100 inches (254cm.) upon a concrete base. The ball shall have a forward deformation of more than .220 of an inch (.56cm.) and less than .290 of an inch (.74cm.) and a return deformation of more than .350 of an inch (89cm.) at 18 lb. (8.165kg.) load. The two deformation figures shall be the averages of three individual readings along three axes of the ball and no two individual readings shall differ by more than .030 of an inch (.08cm.) in each case.

All tests for bound, size and deformation shall be made in accordance with the Regulations in the Appendix hereto.

For play above 4,000 feet (1219m.) in altitude above sea level, two additional types of ball may be used. The first type is identical to those described above except that the bound shall be more than 48 inches (121.92cm.) and less than 53 inches (135cm.) and shall have an internal pressure that is greater than the external pressure. This type of tennis ball is commonly known as a pressurised ball. The second type is identical to tjhose described above except that they shall have a bound of more than 53 inches (135cm.) and less than 58 inches (147cm.) and shall have an internal pressure that is approximately equal to the external pressure and have been acclimatised for 60 days or more at the altitude of the specific tournament. This type of tennis ball is commonly known as a zero-pressure or non-pressurised ball.

All tests for bound, size and deformation shall be made in accordance with the regulations in Appendix 1.

4. The Racket

Rackets failing to comply with the following specifications are not approved for play under the Rules of Tennis:

(a) The hitting surface of the racket shall be flat and consist of a pattern of crossed strings connected to a frame and alternately interlaced or bonded where they cross; and the stringing pattern shall be generally uniform, and in particular not less dense in the centre than in any other area. The strings shall be free of attached objects and protrusions other than those utilised solely and specifically to limit or prevent wear and tear or vibration, and which are reasonable in size and placement for such purposes.

(b) The frame of the racket shall not exceed 32 inches (81.28cm.) in overall length, including the handle and 12.5) inches (31.75cm.) in overall width. The strung surface shall not exceed 15.5) inches (39.37cm.) in overall length, and 11.5) inches (29.21cm.) in overall width.

(c) The frame, including the handle, shall be free of attached objects and devices other than those utilised solely and specifically to limit or prevent wear and tear or vibration, or to distribute weight. Any objects and devices must be reasonable in size and placement for such purposes.

(d) The frame, including the handle, and the strings, shall be free of any device which makes it possible to change materially the shape of the racket, or to change the weight distribution, during the playing of a point.

The International Tennis Federation shall rule on the question of whether any racket or prototype complies with the above specifications or is otherwise approved, or not approved, for play. Such ruling may be undertaken on its own initiative, or upon application by any party with a bona fide interest therein, including any player, equipment manufacturer or National Association or members thereof. Such rulings and applications shall be made in accordance with the applicable Review and Hearing Procedures of the International Tennis Federation, copies of which may be obtained from the office of the Secretary.

Case 1. Can there be more than one set of strings on the hitting surface of a racket?

Decision. No. The rule clearly mentions a pattern, and not patterns, of crossed strings.

Case 2. Is the stringing pattern of a racket considered to be generally uniform and flat if the strings are on more than one plane?

Decision. No.

Case 3. Can a vibration dampening device be placed on the strings of a racket and if so, where can they be placed?

Decision. Yes; but such devices may only be placed outside the pattern of the crossed strings.

5. Server & Receiver

The players shall stand on opposite sides of the net; the player who first delivers the ball shall be called the Server, and the other the Receiver.

Case 1. Does a player, attempting a stroke, lose the point if he crosses an imaginary line in the extension of the net.
    (a) before striking the ball,
    (b) after striking the ball?

Decision. He does not lose the point in either case by crossing the imaginary line and provided he does not enter the lines bounding his opponent's Court (Rule 20(e)). In regard to hindrance, his opponent may ask for the decision of the Umpire under Rules 21 and 25.

Case 2. The Server claims that the Receiver must stand within the lines bounding his Court. Is this necessary?

Decision. No. The Receiver may stand wherever he pleases on his own side of the net.

6. Choice of Ends & Service

The choice of ends and the right to be Server or Receiver in the first game shall be decided by toss. The player winning the toss may choose or require his opponent to choose:-

(a) The right to be Server or Receiver, in which case the other player shall choose the end; or

(b) The end, in which case the other player shall choose the right to be Server or Receiver.

7. The Service

The service shall be delivered in the following manner. Immediately before commencing to serve, the Server shall stand with both feet at rest behind (i.e. further from the net than) the base-line, and within the imaginary continuations of the centre-mark and side-line. The Server shall then project the ball by hand into the air in any direction and before it hits the ground strike it with his racket, and the delivery shall be deemed to have been completed at the moment of the impact of the racket and the ball. A player with the use of only one arm may utilize his racket for the projection.

Case 1. May the Server in a singles game take his stand behind the portion of the base-line between the side-lines of the Singles Court and the Doubles Court?

Decision. No.

Case 2. If a player, when serving, throws up two or more balls instead of one, does he lose that service?

Decision. No. A let should be called, but if the Umpire regards the action as deliberate he may take action under Rule 21.

8. Foot Fault

(a) The Server shall throughout the delivery of the Service:-

(i) Not change his position by walking or running. The Server shall not by slight movements of the feet which do not materially affect the location originally taken up by him, be deemed "to change his position by walking or running".

(ii) Not touch, with either foot, any area other than that behind the base-line within the imaginary extension of the centre-mark and side-lines.

(b) The word "foot" means the extremity of the leg below the ankle.

9. Delivery of Service

(a) In delivering the service, the Server shall stand alternately behind the right and left Courts beginning from the right in every game. If service from a wrong half of the Court occurs and is undetected, all play resulting from such wrong service or services shall stand, but the inaccuracy of station shall be corrected immediately it is discovered.

(b)The ball served shall pass over the net and hit the ground within the Service Court which is diagonally opposite, or upon any line bounding such Court, before the Receiver returns it.

10. Service Fault

The Service is at fault:

(a) If the Server commits any breach of Rules 7, 8 or 9;

(b) If he misses the ball in attempting to strike it;

(c) If the ball served touches a permanent fixture (other than the net, strap or band) before it hits the ground.

Case 1. After throwing a ball up preparatory to serving, the Server decides not to strike at it and catches it instead. Is it a fault?

Decision. No.

Case 2. In serving in a singles game played on a Doubles Court with doubles posts and singles sticks, the ball hits a singles stick and then hits the ground within the lines of the correct Service Court. Is this a fault or a let?

Decision. In serving it is a fault, because the singles stick, the doubles post, and that portion of the net or band between them are permanent fixtures. (Rules 2 and 10, and note to Rule 24.)

11. Second Service

After a fault (if it is the first fault) the Server shall serve again from behind the same half of the Court from which he served that fault, unless the service was from the wrong half, when, in accordance with Rule 9, the Server shall be entitled to one service only from behind the other half.

Case 1. A player serves from a wrong Court. He loses the point and then claims it was a fault because of his wrong station.

Decision. The point stands as played and the next service should be from the correct station according to the score.

Case 2. The point score being 15 all, the Server, by mistake, serves from the left-hand Court. He wins the point. He then serves again from the right-hand Court, delivering a fault. This mistake in station is then discovered. Is he entitled to the previous point? From which Court should he next serve?

Decision. The previous point stands. The next service should be from the left-hand Court, the score being 30/15, and the Server has served one fault.

RULES OF TENNIS

12. When to Serve

The Server shall not serve until the Receiver is ready. If the latter attempts to return the service, he shall be deemed ready. If, however, the Receiver signifies that he is not ready, he may not claim a fault because the ball does not hit the ground within the limits fixed for the service.

13. The Let

In all cases where a let has to be called under the rules, or to provide for an interruption to play, it shall have the following interpretations:-

(a) When called solely in respect of a service that one service only shall be replayed.

(b) When called under any other circumstance, the point shall be replayed.

Case 1. A service is interrupted by some cause outside those defined in Rule 14. Should the service only be replayed?

Decision. No. The whole point must be replayed.

Case 2. If a ball in play becomes broken, should a let be called?

Decision. Yes.

14. The "Let" in Service

The Service is a let:-

(a) If the ball served touches the net, strap or band, and is otherwise good, or, after touching the net, strap or band, touches the Receiver or anything which he wears or carries before hitting the ground.

(b) If a service or a fault is delivered when the Receiver is not ready (see Rule 12).

In case of a let, that particular service shall not count, and the Server shall serve again, but a service let does not annul a previous fault.

15. Order of Service

At the end of the first game the Receiver shall become Server, and the Server Receiver; and so on alternately in all the subsequent games of a match. If a player serves out of turn, the player who ought to have served shall serve as soon as the mistake is discovered, but all points scored before such discovery shall be reckoned. A fault served before such discovery shall not be reckoned. If a game shall have been completed before such discovery, the order of service remains as altered.

16. When Players Change Ends

The players shall change ends at the end of the first, third and every subsequent alternate game of each set, and at the end of each set unless the total number of games is even, in which case the change is not made until the end of the first game of the next set.

If a mistake is made and the correct sequence is not followed the players must take up their correct station as soon as the discovery is made and

follow their original sequence.

17. The Ball in Play

A ball is in play from the moment at which it is delivered in the service. Unless a fault or a let is called it remains in play until the point is decided.

Case 1. A player fails to make a good return. No call is made and the ball remains in play. May his opponent later claim the point after the rally has ended?

Decision. No. The point may not be claimed if the players continue to play after the error has been made, provided the opponent was not hindered.

18. Server Wins Point

The Server wins the point:-

(a) If the ball served, not being a let under Rule 14, touches the Receiver or anything which he wears or carries, before it hits the ground;

(b) If the Receiver otherwise loses the point as provided by Rule 20.

19. Receiver Wins Point

The Receiver wins the point:

(a) If the Server serves two consecutive faults;

(b) If the Server otherwise loses the point as provided by Rule 20.

20. Player Loses Point

A player loses the point if:-

(a) He fails, before the ball in play has hit the ground twice consecutively, to return it directly over the net (except as provided in Rule 24 (a) or (c);) or

(b) He returns the ball in play so that it hits the ground, a permanent fixture, or other object, outside any of the lines which bound his opponent's Court (except as provided in Rule 24 (a) or (c)); or

(c) He volleys the ball and fails to make a good return even when standing outside the Court; or

(d) In playing the ball he deliberately carries or catches it on his racket or deliberately touches it with his racket more than once; or

(e) He or his racket (in his hand or otherwise) or anything which he wears or carries touches the net, posts, single sticks, cord or metal cable, strap or band, or the ground within his opponent's Court at any time while the ball is in play; or

(f) He volleys the ball before it has passed the net; or

(g) The ball in play touches him or anything that he wears or carries, except his racket in his hand or hands; or

(h) He throws his racket at and hits the ball; or

(i) He deliberately and materially changes the shape of his racket during the playing of the point.

Case 1. In serving, the racket flies from the Server's hand and touches the net before the ball has touched the ground. Is this a fault, or does the player lose the point?

Decision. The Server loses the point because his racket touches the net whilst the ball is in play (Rule 20 (e)).

Case 2. In serving, the racket flies from the Server's hand and touches the net after the ball has touched the ground outside the proper court. Is this a fault, or does the player lose the point?

Decision. This is a fault because the ball was out of play when the racket touched the net.

Case 3. A and B are playing against C and D, A is serving to D, C touches the net before the ball touches the ground. A fault is then called because the service falls outside the Service Court. Do C and D lose the point?

Decision. The call "fault" is an erroneous one. C and D had already lost the point before "fault" could be called, because C touched the net whilst the ball was in play (Rule 20(e)).

Case 4. May a player jump over the net into his opponent's Court while the ball is in play and not suffer penalty?

Decision. No. He loses the point. (Rule 20(e)).

Case 5. A cuts the ball just over the net, and it returns to A's side. B, unable to reach the ball, throws his racket and hits the ball. Both racket and ball fall over the net on A's Court. A returns the ball outside of B's Court. Does B win or lose the point?

Decision. B loses the point (Rule 20(e) and (h)).

Case 6. A player standing outside the service Court is struck by a service ball before it has touched the ground. Does he win or lose the point?

Decision. The player struck loses the point (Rule 20(g)), except as provided under Rule 14(a).

Case 7. A player standing outside the Court volleys the ball or catches it in his hand and claims the point because the ball was certainly going out of court.

Decision. In no circumstances can he claim the point:-

(i) If he catches the ball he loses the point under Rule 20(g).

(ii) If he volleys it and makes a bad return he loses the point under Rule 20(c).

(iii) If he volleys it and makes a good return, the rally continues.

21. Player Hinders Opponents

If a player commits any act which hinders his opponent in making a stroke, then, if this is deliberate, he shall lose the point or if involuntary, the point shall be replayed.

Case 1. Is a player liable to a penalty if in making a stroke he touches his opponent?

Decision. No, unless the Umpire deems it necessary to take action under Rule 21.

Case 2. When a ball bounds back over the net, the player concerned may reach over the net in order to play the ball. What is the ruling if the player is hindered from doing this by his opponent?

Decision. In accordance with Rule 21, the Umpire may either award the point to the player hindered, or order the point to be replayed (see also Rule 25).

Case 3. Does an involuntary double hit constitute an act which hinders an opponent within Rule 21?

Decision. No.

22. Ball Falls on Line

A ball falling on a line is regarded as falling in the Court bounded by that line.

23. Ball Touches Permanent Fixtures

If the ball in play touches a permanent fixture (other than the net, posts, singles sticks, cord or metal cable, strap or band) after it has hit the ground, the player who struck it wins the point; if before it hits the ground, his opponent wins the point.

Case 1. A return hits the Umpire or his chair or stand. The player claims that the ball was going into Court.

Decision. He loses the point.

24. A Good Return

It is a good return:-

(a) If the ball touches the net, posts, singles sticks, cord or metal cable, strap or band, provided that it passes over any of them and hits the ground within the Court; or

(b) If the ball, served or returned, hits the ground within the proper Court and rebounds or is blown back over the net, and the player whose turn it is to strike reaches over the net and plays the ball, provided that neither he nor any part of his clothes or racket touches the net, posts, singles sticks, cord or metal cable, strap or band or the ground within his opponent's Court, and that the stroke be otherwise good; or

(c) If the ball is returned outside the posts, or singles sticks, either above or below the level of the top to the net, even though it touches the posts or singles sticks, provided that it hits the ground within the proper Court; or

(d) If a player's racket passes over the net after he has returned the ball, provided the ball passes the net before being played and is properly returned; or

(e) If a player succeeds in returning the ball, served or in play, which strikes a ball lying in the Court.

Note: In a singles match, if, for the sake of convenience, a Doubles Court is equipped with singles sticks for the purpose of a singles game, then the doubles posts and those portions of the net, cord or metal cable and the band outside such singles sticks shall at all times be permanent fixtures, and are not regarded as posts or parts of the net of a singles game.

A return that passes under the net cord between the singles stick and adjacent doubles post without touching either net cord, net or doubles post and falls within the area of play, is a good return.

Case 1. A ball going out of Court hits a net post or singles stick and falls within the lines of the opponent's Court. Is the stroke good?

Decision. If a service: no, under Rule 10(c). If other than a service: yes, under Rule 24(a).

Case 2. Is it a good return if a player returns the ball holding his racket in both hands?

Decision. Yes.

Case 3. The service, or ball in play, strikes a ball lying in the Court. Is the point won or lost thereby?

Decision. No. Play must continue. If it is not clear to the

RULES OF TENNIS

Umpire that the right ball is returned a let should be called.

Case 4. May a player use more than one racket at any time during play?

Decision. No. The whole implication of the Rules is singular.

Case 5. May a player request that a ball or balls lying in his opponent's Court be removed?

Decision. Yes, but not while a ball is in play.

25. Hindrance of a Player

In case a player is hindered in making a stroke by anything not within his control, except a permanent fixture of the Court, or except as provided for in Rule 21, a let shall be called.

Case 1. A spectator gets into the way of a player, who fails to return the ball. May the player then claim a let?

Decision. Yes. If in the Umpire's opinion he was obstructed by circumstances beyond his control, but not if due to permanent fixtures of the Court or the arrangements of the ground.

Case 2. A player is interfered with as in Case No. 1, and the Umpire calls a let. The Server had previously served a fault. Has he the right to two services?

Decision. Yes. As the ball is in play, the point, not merely the stroke, must be replayed as the Rule provides.

Case 3. May a player claim a let under Rule 25 because he thought his opponent was being hindered, and consequently did not expect the ball to be returned?

Decision. No.

Case 4. Is a stroke good when a ball in play hits another ball in the air?

Decision. A let should be called unless the other ball is in the air by the act of one of the players, in which case the Umpire will decide under

Rule 21.

Case 5. If an Umpire or other judge erroneously calls "fault" or "out", and then corrects himself, which of the calls shall prevail?

Decision. A let must be called unless, in the opinion of the Umpire, neither player is hindered in his game, in which case the corrected call shall prevail.

Case 6. If the first ball served - a fault - rebounds, interfering with the Receiver at the time of the second service, may the Receiver claim a let?

Decision. Yes. But if he had an opportunity to remove the ball from the Court and negligently failed to do so, he may not claim a let.

Case 7. Is it a good stroke if the ball touches a stationary or moving object on the Court?

Decision. It is a good stroke unless the stationary object came into Court after the ball was put into play in which case a let must be called. if the ball in play strikes an object moving along or above the surface of the Court a let must be called.

Case 8. What is the ruling if the first service is a fault, the second service correct, and it becomes necessary to call a let either under the provision of Rule 25 or if the Umpire is unable to decide the point?

Decision. The fault shall be annulled and the whole point replayed.

26. Score in a Game

If a player wins his first point, the score is called 15 for that player; on winning his second point, the score is called 30 for that player; on winning his third point, the score is called 40 for that player, and the fourth point won by a player is scored game for that player except as below:-
If both players have won three points, the score is called deuce; and the next point won by a player is scored advantage for that player. If the same player wins the next point, he wins the game; if the other player wins the next point the score is again called deuce; and so on, until a player wins the two points immediately following the score at deuce, when the game is scored for that player.

27. Score in a Set

(a) A player (or players) who first wins six games wins a set; except that he must win by a margin of two games over his opponent and where necessary a set shall be extended until this margin is achieved.

(b) The tie-break system of scoring may be adopted as an alternative to the advantage set system in paragraph (a) of this Rule provided the decision is announced in advance of the match.

In this case, the following Rules shall be effective:
The tie-break shall operate when the score reaches six games all in any set except in the third or fifth set of a three set or five set match respectively when an ordinary advantage set shall be played, unless otherwise decided and announced in advance of the match.

The following system shall be used in a tie-break game.
Singles

(i) A player who first wins seven points shall win the game and the set provided he leads by a margin of two points. If the score reaches six points all the game shall be extended until this margin has been achieved. Numerical scoring shall be used throughout the tie-break game.

(ii) The player whose turn it is to serve shall be the Server for the first point. His opponent shall be

the Server for the second and third points and thereafter each player shall serve alternately for two consecutive points until the winner of the game and set has been decided.

(iii) From the first point, each service shall be delivered alternately from the right and left Courts, beginning from the right Court. If service from a wrong half of the Court occurs and is undetected, all play resulting from such wrong service or services shall stand, but the inaccuracy of station shall be corrected immediately it is discovered.

(iv) Players shall change ends after every six points and at the conclusion of the tie-break game.

(v) The tie-break game shall count as one game for the ball change, except that, if the balls are due to be changed at the beginning of the tie-break, the change shall be delayed until the second game of the following set.

Doubles
In doubles the procedure for singles shall apply. The player whose turn it is to serve shall be the Server for the first point. Thereafter each player shall serve in rotation for two points, in the same order as previously in that set, until the winners of the game and set have been decided.

Rotation of Service
The player (or pair in the case of doubles) who served first in the tie-

RULES OF TENNIS

break game shall receive service in the first game of the following set.

Case 1. At six all the tie-break is played, although it has been decided and announced in advance of the match that an advantage set will be played. Are the points already played counted?

Decision. If the error is discovered before the ball is put in play for the second point, the first point shall count but the error shall be corrected immediately. If the error is . discovered after the ball is put in play for the second point the game shall continue as a tie-break game.

Case 2. At six all, an advantage game is played, although it has been decided and announced in advance of the match that a tie-break will be played. Are the points already played counted?

Decision. If the error is discovered before the ball is put in play for the second point, the first point shall be counted but the error shall be corrected immediately. If the error is discovered after the ball is put in play for the second point an advantage set shall be continued. If the score thereafter reaches eight games all or a higher even number, a tie-break shall be played.

Case 3. If during the tie-break in a doubles game a partner receives out of turn, shall the order of receiving remain as altered until the end of the game?

Decision. If only one point has been played, the order of receiving shall be corrected immediately, and the point already played shall be counted. If the error is discovered after the ball is put in play for the second point, the order of receiving shall remain as altered.

Case 4. If during a tie-break in a singles or doubles game, a player serves out of turn, shall the order of service remain as altered until the end of the game?

Decision. If a player has completed his turn of service the order of service shall remain as altered. If the error is discovered before a player has completed his turn of service the order of service shall be corrected immediately and any points already played shall count.

28. Maximum Number of Sets

The maximum number of sets in a match shall be 5, or, where women take part, 3.

29. Role of Court Officials

In matches where an Umpire is appointed, his decision shall be final; but where a Referee is appointed, an appeal shall lie to him from the decision of an Umpire on a question of law, and in all such cases the decision of the Referee shall be final. In matches where assistants to the Umpire are appointed (Linesmen, Net-cord Judges, Foot-fault Judges) their decisions shall be final on questions of fact except that if in the opinion of an Umpire a clear mistake has been made he shall have the right to change the decision of an assistant or order a let to be played. When such an assistant is unable to give a decision he shall indicate this immediately to the Umpire who shall give a decision. When an Umpire is unable to give a decision on a question of fact he shall order a let to be played.

In *Davis Cup* matches or other team competitions where a Referee is on Court, any decision can be changed by the Referee, who may also instruct an Umpire to order a let to be played.

The Referee, in his discretion, may at any time postpone a match on account of darkness or the condition of the ground or the weather. In any case of postponement the previous score and previous occupancy of Courts shall hold good, unless the Referee and the players unanimously agree otherwise.

Case 1. The Umpire orders a let, but a player claims the point should not be replayed. May the Referee be requested to give a decision?

Decision. Yes. A question of tennis law, that is an issue relating to the application of specific facts, shall first be determined by the Umpire. However, if the Umpire is uncertain or if a player appeals from his determination, then the Referee shall be requested to give a decision, and his decision is final.

Case 2. A ball is called out, but a player claims that the ball was good. May the Referee give a ruling?

Decision. No. This is a question of fact, that is an issue relating to what actually occurred during a specific incident, and the decision of the on-court officials is therefore final.

Case 3. May an Umpire overrule a Linesman at the end of a rally if, in his opinion, a clear mistake has been made during the course of a rally?

Decision. No, unless in his opinion the opponent was hindered. Otherwise an Umpire may only overrule a Linesman if he does so immediately after the mistake has been made.

Case 4. A Linesman calls a ball out. The Umpire was unable to see clearly, although he thought the ball was in. May he overrule the Linesman?

Decision. No. An Umpire may only overrule if he considers that a call was incorrect beyond all reasonable doubt. He may only overrule a ball determined good by a Linesman if he has been able to see a space between the ball and the line; and he may only overrule a ball determined out, or a fault, by a Linesman if he has seen the ball hit the line, or fall inside the line.

Case 5. May a Linesman change his call after the Umpire has given the score?

Decision. Yes. If a Linesman realises he has made an error, he may make a correction provided he does so immediately.

Case 6. A player claims his return shot was good after a Linesman called "out". May the Umpire overrule the Linesman?

Decision. No. An Umpire may never overrule as a result of a protest or an appeal by a player.

RULES OF TENNIS

30. Continuous Play & Rest Periods

Play shall be continuous from the first service until the match is concluded, in accordance with the following provisions:

(a) If the first service is a fault, the second service must be struck by the Server without delay.
The Receiver must play to the reasonable pace of the Server and must be ready to receive when the Server is ready to serve.
When changing ends a maximum of one minute thirty seconds shall elapse from the moment the ball goes out of play at the end of the game to the time the ball is struck for the first point of the next game. The Umpire shall use his discretion when there is interference which makes it impractical for play to be continuous.
The organisers of international circuits and team events recognised by the ITF may determine the time allowed between points, which shall not at any time exceed 30 seconds.

(b) Play shall never be suspended, delayed or interfered with for the purpose of enabling a player to recover his strength, breath, or physical condition. However, in the case of accidental injury, the Umpire may allow a one-time three minute suspension for that injury. The organisers of international circuits and team events recognised by the ITF may extend the one-time suspension period from three minutes to five minutes.

(c) If, through circumstances outside the control of the player, his clothing, footwear or equipment (excluding racket) becomes out of adjustment in such a way that it is impossible or undesirable for him to play on, the Umpire may suspend play while the maladjustment is rectified.

(d) The Umpire may suspend or delay play at any time as may be necessary and appropriate.

(e) After the third set, or when women take part the second set, either player is entitled to a rest, which shall not exceed 10 minutes, or in countries situated between latitude 15 degrees north and latitude 15 degrees south, 45 minutes and furthermore, when necessitated by circumstances not within the control of the players, the Umpire may suspend play for such a period as he may consider necessary. If play is suspended and is not resumed until a later day the rest may be taken only after the third set (or when women take part the second set) of play on such a later day, completion of an unfinished set being counted as one set.
If play is suspended and is not resumed until 10 minutes have elapsed in the same day the rest may be taken only after three consecutive sets have been played without interruption (or when women take part two sets), completion of an unfinished set being counted as one set.
Any nation and/or committee organising a tournament, match or competition, other than the International Tennis Championships (Davis Cup and Federation Cup), is at liberty to modify this provision or omit it from its regulations provided this is announced before the event comences.

(f) A tournament committee has the discretion to decide the time allowed for a warm-up period prior to a match but this may not exceed five minutes and must be announced before the event commences.

(g) When approved point penalty and non-accumulative point penalty systems are in operation, the Umpire shall make his decisions within the terms of those systems.

(h) Upon violation of the principle that play shall be continuous the Umpire may, after giving due warning, disqualify the offender.

31. Coaching

During the playing of a match in a team competition, a player may receive coaching from a captain who is sitting on the court only when he changes ends at the end of a game, but not when he changes ends during a tie-break game.

A player may not receive coaching during the playing of any other match. The provisions of this rule must be strictly construed.

After due warning an offending player may be disqualified. When an approved point penalty system is in operation, the Umpire shall impose penalties according to that system.

Case 1. Should a warning be given, or the player be disqualified, if the coaching is given by signals in an unobtrusive manner?

Decision. The Umpire must take action as soon as he becomes aware that coaching is being given verbally or by signals. If the Umpire is unaware that coaching is being given, a player may draw his attention to the fact that advice is being given.

Case 2. Can a player receive coaching during the ten minute rest in a five set match, or when play is interrupted and he leaves the court?

Decision. Yes. In these circumstances, when the player is not on the court, there is no restriction on coaching.

Note: The word "coaching" includes any advice or instruction.

32. Changing Balls

In cases where balls are to be changed after a specified number of games, if the balls are not changed in the correct sequence, the mistake shall be corrected when the player, or pair in the case of doubles, who should have served with new balls is next due to serve. Thereafter the balls shall be changed so that the number of games between changes shall be that originally agreed.

THE DOUBLES GAME

33. The Doubles Game

The above Rules shall apply to the Doubles Game except as below.

34. The Doubles Court

For the Doubles Game, the Court shall be 36 feet (10.97m.) in width, i.e. 4.5) feet (1.37m.) wider on each side than the Court for the Singles Game, and those portions of the singles side-lines which lie between the two service-lines shall be called the service side-lines. In other respects, the Court shall be similar to that described in Rule 1, but the portions of the singles side-lines between the base-line and service-line on each side of the net may be omitted if desired.

RULES OF TENNIS

35. Order of Service in Doubles

The order of serving shall be decided at the beginning of each set as follows:-

The pair who have to serve in the first game of each set shall decide which partner shall do so and the opposing pair shall decide similarly for the second game. The partner of the player who served in the first game shall serve in the third; the partner of the player who served in the second game shall serve in the fourth, and so on in the same order in all the subsequent games of a set.

Case 1. In doubles, one player does not appear in time to play, and his partner claims to be allowed to play single-handed against the opposing players. May he do so?

Decision. No.

36. Order of Receiving in Doubles

The order of receiving the service shall be decided at the beginning of each set as follows:-
The pair who have to receive the service in the first game shall decide which partner shall receive the first service, and that partner shall continue to receive the first service in every odd game throughout that set. The opposing pair shall likewise decide which partner shall receive the first service in the second game and that partner shall continue to receive the first service in every even game throughout that set. Partners shall receive the service alternately throughout each game.

Case 1. Is it allowable in doubles for the Server's partner or the Receiver's partner to stand in a position that obstructs the view of the Receiver?

Decision. Yes. The Server's partner or the Receiver's partner may take any position on his side of the net in or out of the Court that he wishes.

37. Service Out of Turn in Doubles

If a partner serves out of his turn, the partner who ought to have served shall serve as soon as the mistake is discovered, but all points scored, and any faults served before such discovery, shall be reckoned. If a game shall have been completed before such discovery, the order of service remains as altered.

38. Error in Order of Receiving in Doubles

If during a game the order of receiving the service is changed by the Receivers it shall remain as altered until the end of the game in which the mistake is discovered, but the partners shall resume their original order of receiving in the next game of that set in which they are Receivers of the service.

39.Service Fault in Doubles

The service is a fault as provided for by Rule 10, or if the ball touches the Server's partner or anything which he wears or carries; but if the ball served touches the partner of the Receiver, or anything which he wears or carries, not being a let under Rule 14(a) before it hits the ground, the Server wins the point.

40. Playing the Ball in Doubles

The ball shall be struck alternately by one or other player of the opposing pairs, and if a player touches the ball in play with his racket in contravention of this Rule, his opponents win the point.

Note: Except where otherwise stated, every reference in these Rules to the masculine includes the feminine gender.

APPENDIX 1
REGULATIONS FOR MAKING TESTS SPECIFIED IN RULE 3

(i) Unless otherwise specified all tests shall be made at a temperature of approximately 68° Fahrenheit (20° Centigrade) and a relative humidity of approximately 60 per cent. All balls should be removed from their container and kept at the recognised temperature and humidity when the test is commenced.

(ii) Unless otherwise specified the limits are for a test conducted in an atmospheric pressure resulting in a barometric reading of approximately 30 inches (76cm.)

(iii) Other standards may be fixed for localities where the average temperature, humidity or average barometric pressure at which the game is being played differ materially from 68° Fahrenheit (20° Centigrade), 60 per cent and 30 inches (76cm.) respectively. Applications for such adjusted standards may be made by any National Association to the International Tennis Federation and if approved shall be adopted for such localities.

(iv) In all tests for diameter a ring gauge shal be used consisting of a metal plate, preferably non-corrosive, of a uniform thickness of one-eighth of an inch (.32 cm.) in which there are two circular openings 2.575 inches (6.54cm.) and 2700 inches (6.86cm.) in diameter respectively. The inner surface of the gauge shall have a convex profile with a radius of one-sixteenth of an inch (.16cm.). The ball shall not drop through the smaller opening by its own weight and shall drop through the larger opening by its own weight.

(v) In all tests for deformation conducted under Rule 3, the machine designed by Percy Herbert Stevens and patented in Great Britain under Patent No. 230250, together with the subsequent additions and improvement thereto, including the modifications required to take return deformations, shall be employed or such other machine which is approved by a National Association and gives equivalent readings to the Stevens machine.

(vi) Procedure for carrying out tests:

(a) Pre-compression. Before any ball is tested it shall be steadily compressed by approximately one inch (2.54cm.) on each three diameters at right angles to one another in succession; this process to be caried out three times (nine compressions in all). All tests to be completed within two hours of pre-compression.

(b) Bounded test (as in Rule 3). Measurements are to be taken from the concrete base to the bottom of the ball.

(c) Size test (as in paragraph (vi) above).

(d) Weight test (as in Rule 3).

(e) Deformation test. The ball is placed in position on the modified Stevens machine so that neither platen of the machine is in contact with the cover seam. The contact weight is applied, the pointer and the mark brought level, and the dials set to zero. The test weight equivalent to 18lb. (8.165kg.) is placed on th beam and pressure applied by turning the wheel at a uniform speed so that five seconds elapse from the instant the beam leaves its seat until the pointer is brought level with the mark. When turning ceases the reading is recorded (forward deformation). The wheel is turned again until figure ten is reached on the scale (one inch (2.54cm.) deformation). The wheel is then rotated in the opposite direction at a uniform speed (thus releasing pressure) until the beam pointer again coincides with the mark. Afetr waiting ten seconds the pointer is adjusted to the mark if necessary. The reading is then recorded (return deformation). This procedure is repeated on each ball across the two diameters at right angles to the initial position and to each other.

THIS BOOK HAS SHOWN THE IMPORTANT AND WIDE-RANGING ROLE OF THE COACH. IT HAS ALSO INDICATED THE KNOWLEDGE REQUIRED TO BE AN EFFECTIVE AND SUCCESSFUL COACH. THE SCOPE OF THIS BOOK CANNOT COVER EVERY TOPIC IN DETAIL, SO IF YOU HAVE DEVELOPED AN INTEREST IN SOME ASPECT OF COACHING SUCH AS MENTAL PREPARATION, FITNESS TRAINING OR THE PREVENTION OF INJURY, THE NATIONAL COACHING FOUNDATION, ESTABLISHED TO PROVIDE A SERVICE FOR SPORTS COACHES, RUNS COURSES, PRODUCES STUDY PACKS, BOOKS, VIDEOS AND OTHER RESOURCES ON MANY PERFORMANCE RELATED AREAS PARTICULARLY DESIGNED FOR THE PRACTISING COACH.

CONTACT THE NATIONAL COACHING FOUNDATION AT: 4 COLLEGE CLOSE, BECKETT PARK, LEEDS SL6 3QH
TELEPHONE: LEEDS (0532) 744802